*Resist Turbulent Times: Ways to Save-Our-Selves*
©2024 Verda Harris-Olayinka

Mo' Betta Digital
41 Avenida Fernando Luis Ribas #449
Utuado, Puerto Rico 00641

ISBN: eBook 978-0-9974916-9-2
ISBN: paperback 978-1-7378873-2-4
First edition: January 6, 2024
All rights reserved. No part of this book may be reproduced in any written, electronic, recording or photocopying form without written permission of the author, Verda H. Olayinka or the publisher, Mo' Betta Digital.

Notice of Liability

The information in this book is distributed on an "as is" basis, for informational purposes only, without warranty. While every precaution has been taken in the production of this book, neither the copyright owners nor the publisher shall have any liability to any person or entity with respect to any liability, loss, damage caused or alleged to be caused directly or indirectly by the information contained in this book.

Printed in the USA

Verda Harris-Olayinka

# Resist Turbulent Times: Ways to Save-Our-Selves

# Table of Contents

LIST OF TABLES AND ILLUSTRATIONS ................................ 5
ACKNOWLEDGEMENTS ........................................................ 6
PRELUDE – 1st Edition ............................................................ 7
PREFACE .................................................................................... 8
INTRODUCTION ...................................................................... 13
CHAPTER ONE ......................................................................... 23
   *Setting the Record Straight: Do Not Believe the Hype*
CHAPTER TWO ......................................................................... 43
   *Calling a Thing, a Thing: No Apologies*
CHAPTER THREE ..................................................................... 62
   *Saggin': Beyond Blaming the Victim*
CHAPTER FOUR ........................................................................ 72
   *Melanin Revisited*
CHAPTER FIVE .......................................................................... 87
   *Ethnic Manipulation: A Case Study of Jamaica, Queens County, New York City*
CHAPTER SIX ............................................................................ 104
   *Life in Our Father's House*
CHAPTER SEVEN ...................................................................... 115
   *The Family – Targeted Impacts on the Survival of Our Future Generations*
CHAPTER EIGHT ...................................................................... 130
   *Cultivating Tacticians for Self-Actualization*
CHAPTER NINE ........................................................................ 159
   *Activating Solutions*
CHAPTER TEN .......................................................................... 175
   *Social Situation Surmountable*
AFTERWORD ............................................................................ 186
ABOUT THE AUTHOR ............................................................ 194

# List of tables and illustrations

| Page | Table | |
|---|---|---|
| 25 | | Interactive Timeline of African Civilizations and Greco-Roman/European Histories |
| 52 | 1 | Annual Murder Rates in the U.S. 1990-2022 |
| 65 | 2 | Firearm homicides by age, race, ethnicity, united states 2021 |
| 76 | 3 | Melanin Enhances Our Abilities |
| 82 | 4 | Black Self-Respect |
| 92 | 5 | Queens County Immigrant Population Expansion 2015-2019 |
| 93 | 6 | Total Population, Queens County |
| 117 | 7 | Corona 19 Virus USA 1-2121-2022 through 9-21-2022 |
| 121 | 8 | Education Levels, Jamaica Southeast Queens New York City |
| 123 | 9 | Unemployment Rates USA |
| 123 | 10 | 2.5% Asian Immigrant Unemployment Queens County |
| 132 | 11 | Records of Race Massacres (1863-1877) (13 Years) |
| 140 | 12 | Records of Race Massacres (1918-1923) (5 Years) |
| 143 | 13 | Contemporary Race Massacres |
| 150 | 14 | Total U.S. Population by Race (2022) |

# ACKNOWLEDGEMENTS

The cumulative cells of the ciliate minds energized by the pulsating pineal pinecones which continue to bind our story into one great body of knowledge, combining lifetimes of research and reflection, morphing European infused history into absolute truths empowering us in self-determination to advance bravely and collectively shaping our own destiny:

Harold Cruse
Prof. Njoku Awa
Marcus Garvey
Dr. Josef Ben Jochannan
Dr. John Henrick Clark
Dr. Alain LeRoy Locke
Dr. W.E.B. DuBois
Booker T. Washington
Dr. Ivan Van Sertima
Dr. Maulana Karenga
Dr. Molefi Kete Asante
Haki Madhubuti
Dr. Ronald Braithwaite
Norma J. Goodwin, MD
James Baldwin
Dr. Cornel West
Dr. William E. Cross, Jr.
Dr. Robert L. Harris, Jr.
Dr. James Turner

Dr. Leonard Jeffries
Frances Cress-Welsing, MD
Dr. Marimba Ani
Amiri Baraka
Jawanza Kunjufu
Amos Wilson, MD
Mr. Carol Barnes
Dr. Llaila Afrika
Richard King, MD
Walter Rodney
Kwame Nkrumah
Chancellor Williams
Cheikh Anta Diop
Imhotep Gary Byrd
David Lampel
Iyanla Vanzant
Wayne B. Chandler
Prof. J. Congress Mbata

And many others.

# PRELUDE – 1st Edition

Professor Verda H. Olayinka has given us facts, examples, and activities that will lead to abundance for people to define their own futures.

This book creates a call to action for all people who know the value of self-investment and are willing to learn ways of becoming much better providers for themselves and their families.

This is a must-have book of truth, inspiration, and encouragement and truly the call to activate our unlimited pool of gifts.

I encourage all to add this to their primary reading list.

Professor Dr. Henry G. Miller (1949-2020),
Founder: HGM Energetics Research for World Peace

# PREFACE

On January 6, 2021, the Peoples of the Nation and Peoples of the world witnessed an armed insurrection attempt, giving the appearance of a Massive Mosh Mob of noisy, unconstrained, orgiastic revelry. "Stop the Steal!" "Hang [Vice President] Mike Pence!" Pushing, bumping, slamming–even defecating into the inner sanctions–they made a Massive Mosh Pit of the United States Capitol.

Their "Wall of Death" killed five and injured many, jeopardizing all Senatorial and Legislative Leaders' lives. These demonstrators came packing weapons of war, releasing their anger and hate against the U.S. Government officials. They were sent by former President Donald Trump, and many continue to believe–under false pretenses-with a history of multiple statewide and local counts and recounts that the election was stolen. Many didn't leave the Capitol Grounds until Trump said softly, "Go home and be safe."

Their psychopathic/sociopathic types have generational histories of unchecked, scattered, non-stop massacres and lynchings from the Reconstruction Era to the present that give rise to destructive personalities, sanctioned, and many perpetrated by the police against Kemetic Americans. Their current movement has been largely authorized by the Trump Administration for the purpose of dividing people, and the perpetrators have gone unchecked because radical Republican officials want divisiveness.

Investigators found that current, former, and retired police were present that day. Some of the insurrectionists were wearing Ku Klux Klan outfits, and others were waving swastika posters, both symbols of racism and white supremacy. The number of demonstrators was estimated at 80,000 and only 880 were arrested in 48 states for acts of treason against the United States.

The January 6th investigation panel of the United States House of Representatives completed its task after 18 months. On January 3, 2023, the panel recommended that the Justice Department pursue at least four criminal charges against Trump related to his alleged efforts to thwart the transfer of presidential power:

- Obstruction of an official proceeding
- Conspiracy to defraud the United States
- Conspiracy to make a false statement
- Incitement, rebellion or insurrection

According to the November 18, 2022, CNN Politics broadcast, United States Attorney General Merrick Garland assigned Special Counsel Jack Smith to oversee the criminal investigations into former President Trump's retention of classified documents at his Mar-a-Lago resort home. Special Counsel Smith was assigned to also examine parts of the January 6th insurrection[1].

Trump has inculcated fear and hatred by projecting his nemesis - "one who imposes retribution" from the extension of his name, trumpery. He uses any "strategy calculated to deceive by false show; anything externally splendid but intrinsically of little value; worthless finery." Webster's Unabridged makes this clear!

We witness former President Trump's massive manipulation and deception of his Republican base as they mimic his psychological projection, essentially, against The Constitution of the United States of America. Trump encouraged the "set-up" for 106 House Representatives who joined 17 State Attorneys General to support a Texas lawsuit challenging the election. Former President Trump called Texas Representative Mike Johnson to "spearhead the effort to round up support" for the Texas lawsuit, according to a 12-11-2020 article in the Washington Post.

Imagine the psychological state of all of the American people! White supremacy groups are more predominant, police brutality has become more rampant, and hierarchies in the criminal justice system have become more sophisticated.

---

1  Cohen, Z, Scannell, K., Herb, J., Polantz, K., and Duster, C.. Who is Jack Smith, the special counsel named in the Trump investigations? CNN, November 19, 2022 https://www.cnn.com/2022/11/18/politics/jack-smith-special-counsel/index.html

Republican voters don't want to lose face in the eyes of their political leaders, family members, and neighbors–so they lose faith in a future of true humanity and blindly follow the base at the bottom.

This is occurring at the height of popularity and support for the Black Lives Matter movement. Despite this mental and physical manifestation from without, descendants of Kemet continue to be compelled to reinforce the urgency to plan and work together in various venues to Save-Our-Selves. Active participation eliminates fear and doubt as we reinforce self-confidence while adopting this open-source plan.

Kemetic descendants living in the United States represent the height of character, ethics, and resiliency throughout every life experience. Our Accumulated population from the 2020 census is 89,922,562. This easily estimates up to almost 90 million. With mutual trust, we can collectively plan and execute focused activities to exponentially improve our economic situations. (See Table 14: Total U.S. Population by Race (2022) p.150.)

*Resist Turbulent Times: Ways to Save-Our-Selves* is presently a first edition. It was originally written as the 3rd Edition of Activating Social Solutions: Essential Keys to Progress. The first, published in 2016, was concerned with the killings of George Floyd and others, and assaults against the sons and daughters of Kemet living in America. Events were characterized by marches, demonstrations, and returning home to the same social conditions they left. Published in 2020, the second edition was completed during the Covid-19 national quarantine and just before the attempted insurrection.

*Resist Turbulent Times...*, like the Ghanaian Sankofa tradition, takes us back in our recent history so that we can move forward with informed social realities to Save-Our-Selves. It serves as a coaching tool for solutions specialists to bring together family members, friends and neighbors to plan and execute focused activities collectively and constructively Save-Our-Selves, "One-by-One and All Together."

We live in a period of unrelenting social assaults, appearing to take place in isolated silos scattered throughout the United States, targeting family, friends, and neighbors who may or may not know each other. *The Zulu Personal Declaration*[2] was originally translated in South Africa in 1825. This profound declaration includes the special relationship one has with one's neighbor:

"...My neighbor has a mind;

It, also, comprehends all things,

My neighbor and I have the same origins;

We have the same life-experience and a common destiny;

We are the obverse and reverse sides of one entity;

We are unchanging equals;

We are the faces which see themselves in each other;

We are mutually fulfilling complements;

We are simultaneously legitimate values;

My neighbor's sorrow is my sorrow;

His [Her, Their] joy is my joy.

He [She, They] and I are mutually fulfilled when we stand by each other in moments of need.

His [Her, Their] survival is a precondition of my survival...."

The sociopathic personality behaviors of white supremacists, nationally and globally, have become more sophisticated and entrenched in the belief that covertly and overtly, they can assault us as sons and daughters who are descendants of Ancient Kemet with complete impunity.

---

2    The Zulu Personal Declaration, considered the "quintessential value system of the Zulu people, including what it means to be human." The closest interpretation found on the internet comes from Meserette Kentake. April 21, 2019. Retrieved from https://kentakepage.com/the-zulu-personal-declaration/
It is also referenced by Asante, Molefi K. & Abarry, Abu S. (Eds.). (1996). *African Intellectual Heritage: A Book of Sources*. Philadelphia, PA: Temple University Press, p. 371

I'm referring to the massive harvesting of organs containing our magnificent melanin, mysterious unexplained abductions of children and adult people of color, and fulfilling their objectives within the eugenics plan to exterminate Kemetic/African Americans as part of the global plan for the population reduction of humans on Earth.

Our situation is critical. Without hesitation, *Resist Turbulent Times: Ways to Save-Our-Selves* presents historic social realities leading to a manipulated stagnation, giving rise to the false narrative of all the stereotypes attributed to our so-called arrested development. It serves as a "root cause analysis" of societal actions and efforts that continue to curtail Kemetic progress and how those actions triggered and degraded other events, reducing overall well-being and prosperity.

Saving-Our-Selves, in real time, we use this knowledge to nurture and coach Solution Specialists to embrace our brilliant minds to work with one another and our neighbors. Yes, our mutual prosperity will ensure personal, physical, and spiritual abundance for Our-Selves and our Posterity.

# INTRODUCTION

I had the second edition of this book published in 2020. A few things have changed since I published the book now three years ago. Apart from events on a global stage that called on me to address them in this edition, I discovered there were some copyright issues present in the book that required me to look for a new publisher.

Technically speaking, this should be the third edition of the book, but because of these copyright issues my previous publisher didn't catch, I have changed the title of the book.

Previously titled *Activating Social Solutions: Essential Keys to Progress*, I have now changed the title to *Resist Turbulent Times: Ways to Save-Our-Selves*.

There will still be instances of the old title peppered throughout this book because the concepts remain the same as they relate to that section. There will also be references to this being the third edition. Although I could have edited those references out, it would have meant altering entire sections that followed.

I have been inspired since the nationwide "Occupy" and, more recently, the "Black Lives Matter" Movements to write a book that would present a historical context, reinforce personal and community well-being, motivate personal commitment, and give direction for focused future activities that could bring about social change in various unique settings. It is important to keep in mind that our greatest asset is the 90 million empowered human resource of us working together collectively, and that consensus is our guarantee of survival.

Throughout this book, I refer to Kemet as the ancient name of the continent called Africa, which was named after the Roman Emperor, Africanus. According to Dr. Yosef Ben-Jochannan, the ancient continental mass was also known as Alkebu-Lan or Ta-Meri/Meri-Ta. I prefer to use the name "Kemet"--one of the names for Ancient Egypt. Except when quoting others, I will speak of Negroes, Blacks, African Americans, etc. as Kemetics, sons and daughters of Kemet, evidenced by our inherited bloodlines and DNA via the melanin in our bodies.

*Resist Turbulent Times* rests on the foundation of my cumulative forty years of professional work in the social services, my lifetime role as a scholar of our contemporary experience, and my reflection on the philosophical tenets of Harold Cruse (1916-2005).

Harold Cruse was a great visionary of our time and author of (1967) *The Crisis of the Negro Intellectual* and (1968) *Rebellion or Revolution?* He holds steadfastly to the fact that an individual, family, nation, neighborhood, or community must exist firmly on a tripod of development in politics, economics, and culture.

In *The Crisis*, Cruse drops warnings, instructions, and advice for the "cultural intellectual" in his historical critiques and social analyses of key events that impacted the lives of Kemetic Americans in the 19th and 20th centuries. His writing brought about anger and heated emotional arguments from his intellectual contemporaries in attempts to defend their positions that essentially had not changed the overall conditions for Kemetic Americans. *Rebellion or Revolution?* served as a socialist Marxist critique of leaders and activities before and during the Civil Rights and Black Power Social Movements of the late 1960s.

*Resist Turbulent Times* intends to draw from Cruse's analyses as he attempted to respond to his peers, who piled on critique after critique about the way he wrote, what he wrote, who he wrote about, and how he wrote it. They seemed to be fixated on the form but not the substance of *The Crisis*, which was published during the Civil Rights and Black Power Movements, most blatantly characterized by marches, riots and burning of Black cities.

Interestingly enough is the fact that seventeen years later, in 1984 and again in 2005, *The Crisis* was reprinted in its entirety because the social conditions had not changed. The same continues to be true 56 years after the first printing.

This current strategy of nurturing Solutions Specialists rests on the foundation of Cruse's "Theory of Black Cities," written in *Black World Journal* in January and March 1971 as "Black and White: Outlines of the Next Stage" Parts I and II. Cruse shows us how the mass migrations North, West, and South to the big cities (i.e., more industrialized) following the Reconstruction Period brought about the phenomenon of Black urbanization, which continues to be the main social environment in which our families and children are nurtured and socialized.

Cruse guides us to cultivate flexibility so that we can recognize the unique differences and characteristics in the historical and social development of each Black city. Each urban area has a special role in galvanizing leadership to identify and prioritize key objectives for/with the Solutions Specialists for self-help.

He surmises, "If a group fails for a time to achieve salvation through politics, then economics becomes the next best choice of strategy[3]" (Part II: 17). Cruse urges the cultural intellectual to synthesize a Black social science methodology in the process of developing a functional historical analysis from data that is already available. He challenged Black Studies Programs taught in colleges and universities to include this objective in developing their curricula.

"Black intellectuals have not understood how to synthesize Black cultural factors first with Black historiography and then with the politics and the economics of contemporary Black movements. It is in the area of transformation of social science methodology that the challenge of Black Studies finds its relevance and significance… The key to the cultivation of Black social science (Black Studies) methodology is a new synthesis of Black social data which has already accumulated"(Part I: 70).

Cruse elaborated on his vision for Black Studies Programs in 1971 with "Black Studies: Interpretation, Methodology, and the

---

3    Cruse, H. (1971, March). Black and White Outlines of the Next Stage (pp. 4, 5, 16-19). Black World Magazine

Relationship to Social Movements" in the *Afro-American Studies Journal*. He says that sons and daughters of ancient Kemet residing in America who greatly influence the evolution of Black Cities can serve as social catalysts to expose the central issues and problems that plague American society.

"It is the historic role of black urban movements to point the way to exactly where, in the complex structural organism that is American society, the possible black and white political coalition must direct its organized thrust to bring about, nay, force, constructive social change on behalf of the best interests of all the American people who are deeply perplexed and uneasy over the internal problems of American society" (Cruse: 46).

At the opening of the 21st Century, the National Council for Black Studies put out a call for research papers. I submitted a research article published in the *International Journal of Africana Studies* November/December 2000, 6:1 called, "African Americans and Health Research: Challenges for the New Millennium."

My natural objective was to suggest a plan to implement a network of Africana departments nationwide facilitated by, for example, The National Council for Black Studies, to respond to this universal challenge for optimal mental and physical health in our communities. The article concluded with a quote from Kwame Nkrumah (1963):

"The forces of positive action that are political, economic and cultural need to be mobilized and streamlined for progress. This requires an increase in the number of people contributing to positive action and an improvement in the quality of their contribution. This requires a greater space achieved through positive unity, and it creates an optimum zone of self-induced development[4] "*Consciencism: Philosophy and Ideology for De-Colonization* (Nkrumah, 117).

As mentioned previously, throughout the years of our experience

---

4      Consciencism: Philosophy and Ideology for Decolonization and Development with Particular Reference to African Revolution by Kwame Nkrumah (1963:117)

in the United States, we have used various terminologies to define ourselves from African to Colored, Negro, Black, Afro-American, and African American.

You will see these identities as they relate to quotations of authors I cite throughout the book. I will refer to Kemet's sons and daughters and descendants as empowering all the DNA that we carry in our history, bloodlines, and existence worldwide, from time immemorial to the present, during our sojourns on Earth.

In this special sharing, I would like for us to maintain our well-being. I include meditations for spiritual, internal and external healing. The goal is to incorporate self-help to build internal power, cultivating the necessary inner and outer strength in the process of Saving-Our-Selves.

## Social Science Approach

*Activating Social Solutions* reveals that there is a multidisciplinary way to fully examine the challenges that confront our ability to provide for our basic needs of obtaining food, clothing, and shelter for our families.

My intention is to expose new information to Kemetics in America to attack basic beliefs held by many of us and others who are daily confronted by racism and disenfranchisement:

- We have no history
- We have perpetuated self-hatred via aggression toward ourselves and our families
- We are powerless and innately inferior compared with others
- We need approval by whites to achieve collective goals
- We experience apathy showing lack of interest and unconcern about having a vision for achieving a positive future for ourselves and our children.

For instance, when we examine our lives from the perspective of the social sciences, we find that sociology and psychology are not exclusive ways to see our reality. Soon, a deeper understanding of both reveals that social psychology presents another dimension as we attack that which challenges our growth and development.

The same is true as I intersected the ways in which history, economics, and geography have impacted the political and cultural experiences of Kemetic descendants in America.

Chapter by chapter, I challenge the basic beliefs that play themselves out in the attitudes we display in our behaviors toward ourselves and one another. I seek collectively to motivate our people to act as Solutions Specialists "One-by-One and All-Together" as we strategize plans and actualize immediate activities to Save-Our-Selves and ensure longevity for our future generations.

In Chapter 1, I "set the record straight" using a historical continuum that shows that up until 316 years in the past, which was not so long ago, our Kemetic forefathers were masters. They impacted economic development via trade and commerce throughout Europe, the Middle East, and Indo-China. From now and forever more, we "do not believe the hype" that we are descendants from a "dark continent," which had no significant history besides running through the jungle and swinging from trees. This is just not so!

"Calling a thing, a thing" in Chapter 2, reveals that engraved in the psyches of white America sits an intrinsic hatred for male descendants of Kemet. They have acted out these deep-seated behaviors overtly in rewarding themselves for killing our men and women and reinforcing their basic beliefs triggered by fear, due to the weakness of their own genetic material.

According to Dr. Frances Cress-Welsing, this is fueled by their negative emotions of hate, jealousy and envy, so much so that they legalize institutional support to justify the annihilation of our people. We make "no apologies!" and need not react defensively or offensively to charges of "reverse racism." Black Lives Matter!

Our challenge is mental. How do we strategize and reinforce a plan to Save-Our-Selves? Let's explore this. Fifty years ago, at the conclusion of *The Crisis*, Cruse presented a caveat as a warning about the need to address the social realities of our youth who had become a lost generation.

Chapter 3 examines the reality of "saggin'" that has emerged from the culmination of institutionalized social attacks trying to seal our youth in a permanent state of arrested development. White supremacists have dealt our youth a negative blow by creating a social and psychological image of our youth and reinforcing false accusations via mass media that make it their fault by "blaming the victim" for their actions.

Projection is a psychological defense mechanism where, in this case, many white Americans are so steeped in their own self-hate and impotence that they rationalize generations of their despicable actions of social degradation toward Kemetic Americans. They attempt to reinforce their illusion of white supremacy while flouting behaviors of white privilege. Kemetic descendants who internalize physical and institutionalized aggression from society have acted out with violence toward themselves, their families, and the community. Understanding this reality strengthens us to use our wisdom to actively participate in turning this around.

Race! Not a Theory!!! Throughout the 20th Century, many political, economic, and social decisions have been made into law determined by issues of race. Right now, in the United States, race has evolved into a social albatross that returns to haunt many white people. Conservative political leaders obstinately act out racist behaviors to the detriment of their own constituents.

Race classifications are basically determined by the amount of "melanin" present in our bodies based most prominently on the color of our skin and kinkiness of our hair. Chapter 4 identifies characteristics, which are both scientific and practical. Let's "revisit" this reality of "melanin" to consciously reinforce our internal and external strength, activating these unique biological qualities as we

Save-Our-Selves.

Many ethnic groups immigrate to the United States seeking political asylum. Others enter with support from their own governments and U.S. federal grants to reinforce mutual objectives for economic development. Regardless of race or ethnicity, their presence results in the detriment of opportunities for Kemetic Americans to support themselves and their families in blatant and not-so-blatant ways.

Individuals from other countries are made to believe in the innate inferiority of Kemetic Americans, which continues to be reinforced by mass media. Nationwide, city planning officials enforce racial profiling using strategies of "ethnic manipulation," to bring about gentrification and other objectives that are described in Chapter 5. I use the case study of Jamaica, Queens, NYC to show a series of events that continue to be repeated in neighborhoods and communities throughout the United States.

How do we take this reality out of the isolation of our neighborhoods and collectively maximize a social impact to ensure prosperity for our future generations? "It's all in our state of mind…"

Family is the first social setting we experience when we enter into it at birth. Sociologists consider family to be the primary social institution for human beings because all families exhibit certain behaviors among their members, globally. Many Kemetic Americans have annual family reunions where extended kinship groups share social activities and children become familiar with one another. Extended family ties have become a unique aspect of our culture. However, we have the ability to improve on this.

It is important for us to totally eliminate the toxic violence in our homes, schools, neighborhoods, and communities. We are challenged to consciously reject violence portrayed in the media and not internalize superficial interactions of hatred, jealousy, and deceit, in the guise of reality shows.

My family experience is similar to millions among the 89.9

million Kemetics living in America. "Life in Our Father's House" illustrates in Chapter 6 the roles of millions of fathers everywhere in our population of about 40 million men who are working hard every day to support their families. When we focus internally on our offspring's physical health and safety, an atmosphere of well-being will evolve. We will become better providers for our families, improved guardians of our neighborhoods, and unified protectors of our communities. Let us reaffirm these family and community characteristics while we, acknowledged Generations of U.S. Citizens, step into the role as Solutions Specialists and evolve "One-by-One and All-Together" to collectively Save-Our-Selves.

Social psychologists recommend that we use active participation as an effective strategy for bringing about change. Active participation provides "Solutions Specialists" with opportunities to acquire new information. Chapter 7 serves as a catalyst to change everyone's attitudes, while applying new knowledge and cultivating their communication skills as "tacticians for self-actualization."

We witness key achievements in our efforts to thrive in the urban setting as well as events that continue to take place, preventing long-term achievement. Today, focused active participation will identify more people who believe that we actually *can* work together. We will shift our opinions about trust, and fulfill our intentions to collectively complete projects, and initiate new ones.

Solutions Specialists will refine and reaffirm their roles as leaders as we collectively plan, implement, and complete new projects while training younger community members in unceasing, perpetual motion, continuing the Kemetic objective to Save-Our-Selves. In our communities, Solutions Specialists will bring together those Kemetic Americans who have now become informed, and those who are already aware of our rich history as leaders in trade and economic development. This was the role of our ancestors just prior to their capture and enslavement as prisoners of war.

Again, like Sankofa, we go back a little bit in order to move forward. Kemetic descendants have come full circle in the last 50 years since Civil Rights and Black Power. We avoid making the same mistakes while "activating solutions" in Chapter 8. We see how the movements started, what happened, and the ways the gains were lost again. Ideas for prosumer marketing give readers opportunities to test the economic strategies we can apply in real time. Beware of the antagonists. Always remain level-headed and calm, no matter what or who you encounter. As you can see from Chapter 2, white supremacists will always hate us–they have their own issues.

Always on the higher road, we advance from "becoming" into "being". We are aware of our time and place on planet Earth. We are "activating solutions" to Save-Our-Selves enriched with this knowledge of our past and clearing the smokescreen of recent events. We have arrived at a place where we collectively can control our money. We can keep near and dear to us the 1.4 trillion dollars we generate annually. We can operationalize the social science of economics Right Now! We are ready to adopt strategies and behaviors based on "prosumerism" to "Save-Our-Selves."

# CHAPTER ONE

*Setting the Record Straight: Do Not Believe the Hype*

# Highlights:

I want readers to clear up their beliefs that Kemetic (African) Americans have no history. In truth, our forefathers contributed to World Development for over 10,000 years, just before our great holocaust.

- It is important for our people to realize the "Dark Continent, absent/bereft of history and modern influence," was a big lie.
- This lie was set up and taught as a smoke screen to blind and deceive all peoples of the world about the talents and values our Kemetic ancestors contributed to global social development.
- Most recently, descendants of Africa, the continent named by the Ancients as Al Kebulan, come from a place of more than 1,000 years of socio-political-economic dominance of Europe and Indo-China.
- Our Story shows the greatness of Kemetic Dynasties in a historical continuum, mostly of events in the Common Era (CE), following the Birth of Jesus Christ (BC).

Many books of African American history present readers with a very brief mention of events on the continent of Africa, followed by a great amount of elaboration regarding the capture, the Middle Passage across the Atlantic Ocean, and the slave experience. There might be some references to the Harlem Renaissance prior to elaborating on the Civil Rights and Black Power Movements.

There were basically two schools of thought among African American historians as they wrote and interpreted our history.

Many presented slavery-to-freedom orientation and began with different aspects of the enslavement period others from personal narratives or experiences of well-known individuals, such as Harriet Tubman and the Underground Railroad, or the rebellions of Nat Turner and Denmark Vesey, or even Joseph Cinque, leader of the Amistad mutiny at sea. This style of writing persisted as biographical narratives throughout the early 20th Century.

Kemetic history is to be viewed as a sociological process where peoples of Kemet were forerunners among peoples of the world in their attempt to acquire food, clothing, and shelter. Social organizations evolved to set up geographic control and protection, education of their young, development of science and technology, and support the advancement of religious or spiritual beliefs.

The Social Movements of the late 1960s and early 1970s brought about another group of scholars who sought a more comprehensive interpretation of the Kemetic American experience. Their earlier sources of comprehensive history include the works of J.A. Rogers, Carter G. Woodson, and W.E.B. Dubois, among others. The Neo-Kemetic Scholars, to whom I dedicate this book, advanced historiography by using multiple sources of documentation to refute media images of "Tarzan" and "Jungle Jim," which reinforced commonly held beliefs of a "Dark Continent." These media consistently and falsely propagated untruths, positing that Kemetic Americans had no history prior to the Western influence of the roles of slavery in the Western Hemisphere and colonialism on the continent itself.

Although colonialism had a global impact on indigenous cultures worldwide, this Chapter targets and compares parallel social developments on the continents of Kemet and Europe. It presents us with knowledge of a long historical continuum, which reinforces the fact that we, the descendants of Kemet, have a rich and powerful history. This fact evokes pride when we learn about our accomplishments and contributions to the World in which we live. This historical review begins with the Ancient Egyptian

Civilization, which was eventually overthrown by the Roman Empire in 47 BCE (Before the Common Era) and the conquests of Hannibal in 218 BCE, leading to the Common Era-CE (after the Death of Christ AD).

## Interactive Timeline of African Civilizations and Greco-Roman/European Histories

This timeline shows the overlapping histories of Kemetic (African) and Greco-Roman / European civilizations. Go to the year or Century of interest. Click on the event to see the full description.

Source: http://www.tikitoki.com/ timeline/entry/678688/Timelin e-ofAfricanCivilizations-and-GrecoRomanEuropean Histories/

Students of Kemetic history will then become aware of significant events that occurred throughout the Common Era leading to the demise of the Great Songhai Empire whose people continued to engage in armed struggle through 1700, about 80 years after a significant number of prisoners of war were brought to the Colonial North American Village of Jamestown, Virginia in 1619. The Songhai fought against Arabs and Muslims, who helped Europeans establish global colonialism. Colonialism parallels the slave interlude in the Americas and ends in the 1960s.

These changes were influenced by the introduction of gunpowder as a weapon, the invention of superior ships fueled by wind, not humans using oars, and the emergence and value of human trafficking to provide free labor as a major contribution to the rapid growth and development in the United States. It is important for students of history to maintain their focus that slavery in the Americas represents a very short episode in Kemetic's long history.

Referring to the "Holocaust of Enslavement," Maulana Karenga, (1993:115) writes, "If one objectively calculates the costs to Africa and Africans in terms of the 50 to 100 million lives lost through mass murder, war, the forcible transfer of populations, and the brutal rigors of the Middle Passage, and of enslavement as well as the dehumanization and cultural destruction, one cannot help but conclude that of all the holocausts of history, none surpasses this one."

As comparative markers, this opening chapter compares key social developmental events from ancient Egyptian Civilization which was eventually overthrown by the Roman Empire (47 BCE). Hannibal, the Great Kemetic General from Carthage marched through Spain and Gaul (present-day France), traveling over the Alps in 218 BCE while Egypt was still in power. Carthage is located in present-day Tunisia, a country on the North African border between present-day Algeria and Libya bordering the Mediterranean Sea, just South of the Island of Sicily.

Rome was eventually conquered in 476 AD when the Germanic general Odoacer or Odovacar overthrew the last of the Roman Emperors, Augustus Romulus. About 200 years later, the Kemetic Moorish Civilization emerged to influence Spain and other countries in Europe for approximately 800 years from 711 to 1500 CE.

In medieval Europe, rural life was governed by a system scholars call "feudalism." In a feudal society, the king granted large pieces of land called fiefs to noblemen and bishops. Landless peasants, known as serfs, did most of the work on the fiefs. The Catholic Church ruled most of Europe during the early Middle Ages and many small feudal kingdoms and their inhabitants were required to tithe 10% of their earnings to the Church, receiving in return protection from bandits and thieves.

Pope Leo III appointed Charlemagne, who never fought wars or conquered kingdoms, to be the "Emperor" of Christian Europe. Areas of Roman influence later became defined as the Holy Roman

Empire in 800 CE. The Crusades began in 1096, when Pope Urban summoned a Christian army to fight its way to Jerusalem, and the war continued on and off until 1303 when the defeated Crusaders retreated back to Europe after fighting 200 years in nine different campaigns. Many thousands of people from both sides lost their lives and the Muslims held on to the territory called the Holy Land in the eastern Mediterranean[5].

These centuries parallel simultaneous events during the Ghana Civilization which lasted approximately 787 years, from 300 CE to 1087 CE and the Mali Empire for 200 years, from 1230 to 1468 CE, when Sunni Ali Ber recaptured Timbuktu from Mali. He established the Songhai Empire for 123 years between 1464 and 1591 CE when a Moroccan army set out to attack Songhai. Smaller factions of the Songhai army continued their resistance against Arabs and Europeans through 1690.

## Definitions and Terminologies

Let us begin with a clear definition of what we mean by civilization. According to Webster, acquiring the status of civilization requires that a nation or unified people are composed of social organization of a high order and meet the following criteria:

- Advances in the Arts, Science, etc.
- The total culture of a people, nation, or period
- The countries and peoples are considered to have reached a high stage of social and cultural development.

Civilizations require a specific system of laws to support an advanced political system for control and protection, an economic system to provide food and shelter for the people, a religious system for moral development, and education for the training of the young. The civilizations that became dominant committed war and conquest against neighboring kingdoms for taxation and political power and control.

---

5      https://www.historycrunch.com

## Definition of Empire:

1. Supreme power in governing, dominion, sovereignty; absolute power or authority
2. Government by an emperor or empress
3. The period during which such a government prevails
4. The territories, regions, or countries under the jurisdiction and dominion of an emperor or empress
5. Generally, empires are established through superior weapons in war, plundering, or other acts of aggression against smaller states or territories.

Eventually, all empires experienced a demise and end over time due mostly to external aggression of neighboring kingdoms resisting subjugation and competing for political dominance, wealth, power, and geographic control.

Emperors must establish and maintain a massive military. A clear order of command must be enforced for planning and carrying out military tactics, i.e., general, captain, and lieutenant. Coordinated civilian support must be highly entrenched to outfit a marching army. This includes the supplies and the maintenance of open supply lines to ensure the success of every land or sea battle or skirmishes against local civilian takeover.

These activities include the resources to fund the continued manufacture of weapons, shields, uniforms, helmets, shoes, sandals, and boots. Civilian skills would include farming, cloth weaving, sewing, shoe making, designers of chariots, wagons, ships, and other vehicles, obtaining and refining local materials, and metallurgy of copper, bronze, and iron for the design and manufacture of weapons. Animals such as horses or elephants would have to be raised and battle-trained to transport supplies and food for animals and men.

An equally proportional medical team would be trained in the use of herbs and other healing methods to tend to wounded soldiers. Portions of the same military are required to maintain local control with the collection of taxes, fine cloths and spices, and oversee mining for local gold and other precious stones to placate the Emperor or Empress and their retinue. To date, most of the history on planet Earth is written in terms of war and conquest. The size of conquering armies can provide us with the level and implied sophistication of each Empire as we progress through the centuries.

Ancient History in the Land called Ta-Merry, Kemet later named Egypt – On the Continent, Al-Kebulan

Kemetic astronomers used a calendar of the stars that incorporated 365 ¼ days as far back as 10,000 years. They used advanced knowledge of geometry and trigonometry to arrive at such an accurate calculation. The people evolved from being hunters and gatherers to becoming more sedentary by farming and raising crops. Early people of Kemet began to live in large communities whose leaders established agreements to come together as states.

Around 4000 BCE, the multiple states eventually expanded their rule as empires in Ethiopia, Kush and Egypt, and they began using a calendar that was refined to incorporate 365 ¼ days. The inhabitants developed skills in visual art, evidenced by cave paintings and sculptures carved out of rock. Developing a system of hieroglyphic writing in pictures and symbols was another early technology that evolved then, facilitating the writing of the Egyptian Book of the Dead.

The polytheistic religion of the ancient Egyptians fueled the development of their mysteries system, which served as a foundation for an advanced education system. From the age of seven, young boys and girls were chosen to be trained as priests and priestesses. They developed a 40-year curriculum in the temples where students learned science, mathematics, architecture, religion and magic. Children were trained as artists and scribes to write on stone, wood, and papyrus paper made from wood. Located in Thebes, the Grand Lodge of Luxor represented the greatest achievement as a library and place of learning.

Imhotep served as the first recorded doctor under Pharaoh Djoser around 2800 BCE. He also had roles as Prime Minister, architect, and poet. Five hundred years later, Imhotep became known as the God of Medicine, and the Temple of Imhotep became humankind's first hospital.

The people of Egypt built the temples and pyramids as public works projects during the annual four-month period when the flooded Nile River would cover fertile farmland. Thousands of people were called upon to help while they had nothing to do until the river was expected to recede. Sometimes, it took an excess of 100 years to complete the building of a great pyramid.

Pharaoh Akhenaton lived from 1373 to 1357 BCE, and he was most famous for teaching his people to revert from polytheism to the worship of one God. He wrote books and poems about the God Amen-Ra and introduced the idea of God as a trinity of Love, Soul, and Body/Life. He ordered massive temples to be erected in the city of Akhenaton with stories on the wall, written in hieroglyphs about the spiritual traits of Amen-Ra.

The people of ancient Kemet were always under the fear of being attacked by the Hyksos, their enemies from Asia and the Kushite Ethiopians from the South. The Kemetic bronze weapons were eventually no match for the iron weapons of the Hyksos and other enemies. The Romans finally conquered Egypt when Roman Emperor Anthony killed Cleopatra VII in 47 BCE.

## Kemetic General Hannibal and the 2nd Carthaginian War

Hannibal, born in 247 BCE, was the son of General Hamilcar Barca, who was defeated by Rome in the first Carthaginian War. Barca taught Hannibal all he knew about war and conquest. In 221 B.C., Hannibal was given command of an army when he was 26. Hannibal established control of Iberia (present-day Spain) by marrying the Princess Imilce and either conquered or created alliances with smaller Iberian kingdoms. The seaport city of Cartagena is where he established residence. In late spring, 218 B.C., Hannibal marched through the Pyrenees Mountain Range toward Gaul (southern France) with more than 100,000 troops and 37 war elephants.

His army eluded Roman General Scipio by crossing Gaul's Rhone River ahead of Scipio's planned confrontation and continued on to cross the Alps in spite of local resistance of guerrilla attacks of indigenous tribes. On the 15th day of the crossing, and more than five months away from Cartagena, Hannibal finally exited the Alps with just 20,000 in the infantry, 6,000 in the cavalry and all 37 elephants. This continues to be considered a remarkable military achievement.

For three years, Hannibal's army fought against Scipio in Italy inflicting heavy losses on Rome at a heavy cost of men and elephants, resulting in a stalemate just three miles from Rome. Eventually, in 203 BCE Rome changed tactics and sent armies to attack Iberia and march on to Carthage forcing Hannibal to abort the Roman campaign, and return to defend Carthage. Hannibal lost the Battle of Zama due to Rome's larger and better-equipped military. The Romans used the sound of trumpets to stampede the elephants, causing them to circle back trampling the Carthaginian troops.

## The Ghana Empire

Around 300 CE, ancient Ghana achieved status as a state after bringing together nearby kingdoms under its dominion. Geographically, Ghana was located on the West coast of Al-Kebulan, also known as the Gold Coast. It became known as the Land of Gold by merchants and traders along the Trans-Saharan Trade Route. Ancient Ghana also had a trade monopoly on salt by controlling the salt mines in the city of Taghaza. Ghana maintained its wealth by controlling trade, levying import and export taxes on the traders along two main trade routes— North to Morocco and Libya and West to the Bornu region near Lake Chad.

The capital, Kumbi Saleh, was strategically divided into two sections, one for the Tunka (King) and the ancient Ghanaians and the other section of the city for all other immigrants including Muslim traders, after 711 CE. By 1065, Tunka Menin began to realize that there was a greater influx of Muslim traders entering the region, so he "showed political and economic wisdom by appointing several Muslims as Ministers, allowing them to practice their religion freely"(Karenga, 92). The Tunka was able to maintain harmonious relations by maintaining peace in the Empire and he gained access to the northern Saharan trade routes. Tunka Menin was an absolute monarch and held an elaborate court that included counselors, ministers, interpreters, and a treasurer. He maintained a standing army of 200,000, of which more than 40,000 were bowmen.

"At the peak of its empire, ancient Ghana contained a population of several million and a territory of about 250,000 square miles"(Karenga, 92). Ghana utilized good public administration to maintain harmony and control local revolts. Merchants in the ancient Ghana Empire purchased salt, daggers, silk, jewelry, timepieces, and fine cloth from other parts of Sudan. They also traded bars of iron, gold, leather, cotton, kola nuts, shea butter, millet and sorghum. This growth, development, and domination of the Ghana Empire continued for approximately 776 years.

In 1076, Almoravids, who were religious reformers, engaged a Berber army that captured the Ghanaian capital city, Kumbi Saleh. The Almoravids eventually lost control of the Empire and by 1087 CE, the empire disintegrated into smaller states. This laid the foundation for the rise of Mali.

## The Mali Empire

It took about 143 years for Kangaba, which was a small state in the Ghana Empire, to nurture Sundiata, who defeated competing enemies and brought together local kingdoms, establishing himself as Emperor in about 1230 CE. He created the capital city of Niani as a trading hub and financial base as he established control of the

Trans-Saharan Trade Route. Sundiata created the richest farming area in the West with the development of the agriculture industry when he encouraged former soldiers to engage thusly during peacetime. Twenty-five years of his leadership ended with his death in 1255 CE.

Mansa (Emperor) Musa ascended to the throne in 1312 CE, and in 20 years of his rule, Mali doubled the geographic expanse of the Ghana Empire. Mansa Musa conquered most of the major Berber cities of the western desert and stretched its supremacy into the area presently known as Mauritania and southern Algeria, to the far South into Hausa land– presently northern Nigeria, and East to Lake Chad. The population within the domain of the Mali Empire increased to approximately 10 million inhabitants.

1325 CE brought about an unprecedented event in African Muslim history. Mansa Musa paid for his hajj to Mecca and Medina, located in present-day Saudi Arabia, by bringing 80 to 100 camel loads of gold dust. Accompanying Mansa Musa were "60,000 individuals, majority soldiers, baggage men, and royal secretaries to record the momentous trip"(Karenga, 94). His retinue included friends, doctors, teachers, and local political leaders.

The Sultan of Cairo honored Mansa Musa and provided him with "royal assistance for the remainder of his trip." It is said that Mansa Musa depressed the price of gold for twelve years as a result of the gifts distributed in Cairo. On his return trip, he convinced scholars, jurists, architects, and skilled men from Cairo, Mecca, Medina, and Tripoli, as well as African scholars from the University of Fez in Morocco, to accompany him back to Niani. As-Seheli, a Moor, poet and architect from Grenada, Spain, returned with Mansa Musa to construct his palace and a number of mosques in Mali. He also constructed the University of Sankore in Timbuktu, which became an intellectual center that attracted students and professors throughout the Muslim World" (Karenga, 94).

Mansa Musa laid the basis for European recognition and respect South of the Sahara because scholars and traders who traveled shared the presence of the Empire throughout the world. Although Mali was beginning to decline in 1400, in 1494, the Portuguese sought and established diplomatic relations and exchanged ambassadors with Mali. Songhai started to establish its imperial hegemony in 1468.

### The Songhai Empire: Pre-Colonial Kemet

Sunni Ali Ber was a powerful tyrant who captured Timbuktu from Mali in 1468 CE, four years after he became a ruler in 1464. He spent most of his time marching in aggressive conquest, conquering local kingdoms, building up his army and increasing the size of his cavalry. Prior to his death in 1492 CE, he expanded the Empire, providing a foundation for remarkable greatness to take place in the Empire.

Askia Muhammed assumed the throne as Emperor of the Songhai Empire in 1493, where he ruled for 36 years until 1529. Askia built the most expansive and organized Empire by surrounding himself with top leaders and rich residents of the major cities of Gao (10,000 inhabitants), a caravan center for trade around the world, Timbuktu (population 100,000 in 1450 and where scholars numbered 25,000) and Jenne, on an island in the Niger River and accessible only by water. He appointed governors to be administrators when he divided the kingdom into several provinces.

Emperor Askia Muhammed attracted international attention when he made his Hajj to Mecca in 1495, three years after Columbus sailed on his first voyage to America.

Askia Muhammed brought 300,000 pieces of gold to support his expenses, provide generous gifts, and to support the acquisition of items from local merchants. He took 5,000 horsemen and 1,000 foot soldiers. Askia solidified his political association with Muslims throughout Kemet when he accepted the appointment as Caliph of the Western Sudan, a title conferred upon him by the Sharif of Mecca, the Spiritual Leader of all Islam.

Universities, libraries, and schools were erected in the cities of Gao, Jenne, and Timbuktu. They taught philosophy, law, government, astronomy, mathematics, medicine, literature, ethnography, hygiene, logic, rhetoric, grammar, geography, music, and poetry writing. Askia developed a school system that prepared young people for college.

Askia the Great ruled for 35 years until his son removed him from office in 1528, and he died ten years later. Weak leaders and short rules led to internal fighting, which influenced social, political, and economic strife. Many of the conquered states revolted against Songhai and external countries attacked the Empire. In 1594, the Sultan of Morocco, armed with guns and a cannon, captured the salt mines at Taghaza and the gold mines near the city of Niani. The Songhai forces fought their enemies for more than 70 years. Armies of Islam continued to march against the traditional African kingdoms. These little wars paved the way for Arabs and Muslims to acquire money and guns to sell African prisoners of war into slavery.

### Kemetic Moorish Empire in Spain

The Spanish occupation by the Moors began in 711 CE when a Kemetic army, under their leader Tariq ibn-Ziyad, crossed the Strait of Gibraltar from northern Kemet and invaded the Iberian Peninsula 'Andalus' (Spain under the Visigoths-Germans). A European scholar sympathetic to the Spaniards remembered the conquest in this way:

"The reins of their (Moors) horses were as fire, their faces black as pitch, their eyes shone like burning candles, their horses were swift as leopards and the riders fiercer than a wolf in a sheepfold at night . . . The noble Goths [the German rulers of Spain to whom Roderick belonged] were broken in an hour, quicker than tongue can tell. Oh, luckless Spain!"

At its height, Cordova, the heart of Moorish territory in Spain, was the most modern city in Europe. The streets were well-paved, with raised sidewalks for pedestrians. During the night, ten miles of streets were well illuminated by lamps. (This was hundreds of years before there was a paved street in Paris or a street lamp in London). Cordova had 900 public baths-we are told that a poor Moor would go without bread rather than soap!

The Moors are credited with utilizing their knowledge and expertise to bring about a more leisurely life in Spain and acting as a catalyst for introducing key innovations that facilitated development. The Moors brought skills in farming and animal husbandry, rice, strawberries, cotton, sugar cane, ginger, lemons and dates (Karenga, 99). "As first-rate engineers, the Moors built Spain its first aqueduct system for irrigation, its reservoirs for water, underground silos for grain, tunnels through mountains, raised sidewalks, lighted paved streets and dams."

In addition, they built a sewer system and artificial lakes to beautify cities. In areas of mining and manufacturing, they mined gold, silver, copper, tin, lead, iron and alum, creating both luxury and utilitarian items. The Moors introduced cotton manufacturing to Europe. They enhanced shipbuilding and dominated trade and maritime commerce with other Muslims on the Mediterranean Sea up to the 12th Century.

Where architecture was concerned, the Moors' focus was beauty and functionality. In the 10th Century, the city of Cordova boasted of "10,000 palaces of the wealthy and many royal palaces with exquisitely designed gardens" (Karenga, 100). There were 900 beautiful public baths and many private ones at a time when the rest of Europe considered bathing to be self-indulgent and a sin.

The Moors made education universal at a time when even European kings could not read or write, and 99% of Christian Europe were illiterate. In the 10th and 11th Centuries, when Europe had no public libraries and only two significant universities, the Moors gave Spain more than 70 public libraries and the one in Cordova housed 600,000 manuscripts. They built 17 famous universities in Spain in Almeria, Cordova, Granada, Juen, Malaga,

Seville, and Toledo, and established an observatory at Seville.

Knowledge of the Arabic language was viewed as a key to scholarship. Astronomy, physics, chemistry, geometry, philology, geography, and mathematics were subjects taught in the universities. Other topics included trigonometry, botany, and history. Students from Kemet, the Middle East, and Europe came in vast numbers to attend these classes. Women were accepted as students and they were encouraged to engage in serious study. They also moved freely in public and engaged in various gatherings.

"Approximately 400 years before Magellan's trip in 1519 established for Europe that the world was round, the Moors taught it in geometry class using a globe. In fact, El Idrisi, a Moor, wrote a book in the mid-twelfth century observing that according to astronomers and other learned men and philosophers, 'the world is round as a sphere.' He also suggested a concept of gravity, stating in his book that the earth, "draws to itself all that is heavy in the same way a magnet attracts iron" (Karenga,101).

The Moors maintained political dominion and control of Spain for almost 800 years. They played a major role in bringing culture and science to aid in the internal development of the country and its people. Queen Isabella and King Ferdinand ordered their forces to attack Grenada in 1492. This event marks the demise of the Moorish Empire in Spain. Isabella and Ferdinand used the wealth they obtained from sacking Grenada to fund the first voyage of Christopher Columbus to the Americas when he found that Africans had already preceded him. (Van Sertima, 1976:11)

The Christian Inquisition in Spain condemned science, closed the universities, decreased the number of looms in Seville by four-fifths, and destroyed all the baths in a hysterical drive against imagined sin. This resulted in overall decay throughout Spain (Karenga,102).

## Kemetic Explorers Cross the Atlantic Ocean

Further research will reveal much evidence of Kemetic crossings of the Atlantic Ocean centuries before the Columbus voyages. These historic events were thoroughly researched by Dr. Ivan Van Sertima (1935-2009) in the seminal (1976) *African Presence in Ancient America: They Came Before Columbus*. We return to the 14th Century Mali Empire when the borders were secure, diplomatic relationships with the Muslim Traders were intact and the immediate objective was maintaining the status quo.

Abubakari, the second grandson of the daughter of Sundiata, had risen to the throne and was bored with the tedium of just holding court and making imperial decisions. By 1310 CE he began to share a boyhood dream with his ministers about his deep curiosity and desire to know what was on the other side of the Great Water. He became obsessed with making plans for such a journey and listened to all the tales of the sea.

Emperor Abubakari met and conferred with the boatmen who spent generations navigating the three main rivers: Niger, the Gambia and Senegal. These rivers served as transportation routes for trading and ferrying residents to major cities and villages along the banks. Word of boats that traveled along the East African coasts of the Indian Ocean came back from as far East as Lake Chad.

He decided to diversify the designs they recommended by ordering the building of different ships, with some driven by wind with sails, some powered by men using oars and some incorporating both designs. As a leading edge, Abubakari sent a fleet of two hundred ships each with an accompanying supply ship carrying provisions of dried meat and grain, gifts, trade items, and gold. He ordered his captains not to return unless they "reach the end of the ocean or exhausted your food and water" (Van Sertima, 45).

After a very long wait, the captain of a ship that was the last of the fleet returned. He reported that he turned his ship around when he saw the others being drawn by a very swift current and disappearing over the horizon. Abubakari became even more determined to follow his dream. Similar to traveling on the Great Sahara Desert they would use an ancient compass and the stars at night to ensure direction; they stored fruit in huge ceramic jars; and the ships would communicate with each other using the talking drum.

In 1311, Abubakari conferred power to his brother, Mansa (Emperor) Kankan Musa in case Abu did not return within a reasonable amount of time. Accompanied by his Griot and a huge retinue of men and women, Abubakari, "dressed in a flowing white robe"(Van Sertima, 48), led a fleet of 200 ships down the Senegal River to points West across the Great Water now known as the Atlantic Ocean.

The Quetzalcoatl people of the Mexican Valley were expecting the arrival of a messenger from the land of the burnt sun who was prophesied by the Toltec diviners to take place in 1311, "six cycles according to the Toltec calendar, after Quetzalcoatl, their spiritual leader, disappeared from among the Toltecs at Tula" (Van Sertima, 72). The people were drawn to the shore when they heard the drums from 200 announcing the arrival of their Emperor, Abubakari, from Mali. The sound of the drums reached them from across the ocean long before the sight of Abubakari in a flowing white robe, standing on a huge raised platform in the center of the lead ship surrounded by "boats drifting out of the East like a shoal of sea dragons"(Van Sertima, 71). Imagine the pride and joy of fulfillment and accomplishment in the heart and mind of Emperor Abubakari.

The two cultures experienced mutual adaptations when they interacted by sharing foods and religious ceremonies. Abubakari and his people from Mali did not come to take gold. They brought gold. His learned scholars, medicine men, philosophers and scientists from the Universities of Timbuktu and Niani shared knowledge with the wise Toltec men and women leaders and among the Quetzalcoatl people in true intercultural communication.

## Kemetics of Industry, Knowledge and Power

The objective of this introductory chapter is to dispel the myths held by most Americans that descendants of Kemet (Africa) have no history and have not contributed to world development. The history of warrior kings and empires does not rest solely with the Kemetic Empires but permeated human interactions from the Roman Empire through medieval Europe and Kemet, the Turkish Ottoman Empire 1299-1699, and the British Empire 1699-1901.

A review of the 1,151 cumulative years of control of economic development by the Ghana, Mali, and Songhai Empires provides us with knowledge of their extensive influence and exposure during trade throughout the Mediterranean border states of Egypt, Morocco, Libya, Tunisia also known as (aka) Carthage, Spain, Gaul aka France, Italy, and Arabia. The awareness of the presence of gold in the Gold Coast and the salt mines at Taghaza drew the envy of multiple kingdoms. Resentment of invasion, occupation and its resulting empirical control of many of the kingdoms would likely increase the anger of the smaller ruling bodies and the recently maturing ruling kingdoms in Europe.

## Final Demise of Kemetic Empires

Armies of the Songhai Empire continued to fight for 70 years until 1664 (45 years after Jamestown) after the Moroccan army, using guns and cannons as superior weapons, captured the salt mines at Taghaza and the gold mines near the city of Niani. The African population held in bondage, taken as prisoners of war in early Colonial North America, increased in 20 years from 6,971 in 1680 to 27,817 by 1700. (Painter, 24)

In retrospect, let's consider strategies of war to be similar to a game of chess. The pawns as foot soldiers and knights as cavalry engage in battle to protect the Queen and King, educated, artisans, wealthy residents, women and children of the kingdom. Essentially, they were the prisoners of war who were captured and brought to the Americas. They were valued individuals for their ability to provide free labor and many were already skilled in certain crafts.

Skilled craftsmen included but were not limited to iron workers, carpenters, masons, bricklayers, shipbuilders, herbalists and curative scientists. They used their problem-solving intellect to contribute to the rapid growth and development of the United States for more than 321 years, of which free labor counted for more than 244 years since 1619. The impact of forced labor continues to have residual socio-economic effects on Descendants of Kemet to this day.

"Capitalism could not have been built without the systematic exploitation and oppression of the working class, including, crucially, the super-exploitation and special oppression of Black slaves and their descendants. Right up to the present day, American capitalism depends on racism both materially, for the profits it generates, and ideologically, for the divisions it creates within the working class." (1985: D. Roberts)

Our family oral histories were accurate when they impressed upon us that we were the descendant sons and daughters of kings and queens. No longer will we allow descendants of Kemet living in America to be minimized in thought, word, or deed.

# SOURCES

*The Black Man of the Nile and His Family*
Ben-Jochannan, Y. (1981). Alkebu-lan Books and Education Materials: New York.

*African-American Studies for the Adult Basic Reader*
Harris, V.L. (1986). MAC/AEA Adult Literacy Program Staff Development Mini- Grant Project, Office of Academic Affairs, City University of New York.

*Introduction to Black Studies, 2nd Ed.*
Karenga, M. (1993). The University of Sankore Press: Los Angeles.

*Creating Black Americans*
Painter, N. (2007). Oxford University Press: New York.

*The African Presence in Ancient America: They Came Before Columbus.*
Van Sertima, I. (1976). Random House: New York.

*A System Built on Slavery*
Roberts, D. (1985). SocialistWorker.Org. Retrieved October 12, 2016, from https://socialistworker.org/series/The-History-of-Black-America.com

www.britannica.com/place/Timbuktu-Mali

www.britannica.com/place/Holy-Roman-Empire

# CHAPTER TWO

*Calling a Thing, a Thing: No Apologies*

## Highlights:

- Deep within the psyches of American men of power and influence lies a hatred of the Kemetic descendant Male… And you can't change that!
- The police, the Grand Jury, and their local enforcers have replaced the hooded KKK and brought their hidden identities into the open, protected by a law codified by legislative double-speak.
- Their sport has always been the public killing of our men and boys with impunity. They receive no punishment for their crimes.
- Theirs is an innate envy of Kemetic genetic material, resulting in a psychological defense mechanism against fear and hate resolved the moment they pull the trigger.

There is a link between art and the events that are going on around us. It may attract the eye or the ear. Spoken word, sound or movement and the artistic creation is nurtured and produced by the creator who sends it out to somehow impact the observer. The artist may write a song to make the audience laugh or cry, feel good or bad, or even become aggressive or passive. The ones who see or experience the artistic product may have no conscious reaction at all. Very often, we store it in our subconscious minds where the feelings and thoughts linger, making a quiet, ongoing impression on the ways we see and act in the world where we live.

These creative products can get grouped together by a producer, similar to songs that we select on a CD or MP4, to create a certain mood at a particular time and space. An editor puts a group of poems or short stories together for the reader to experience ideas and feelings as they go through the book. We are most familiar with experiencing the work of a band leader who brings together other musicians to make sound and rhythm to create harmony or dis-harmony for this musical presentation and a vocalist who weaves a story with the lyrics.

A dance choreographer combines the visual movement of other dancers and sound. These can be teamed with color to bring about different sensations and feelings in the minds of the audience. The director of a play or movie combines the scenery, background music and costumes, and guides actors to draw audiences into the story. A curator combines art pieces in an art exhibition, starting with a visual concept or set of ideas where they want to instill different feelings and sensations in the minds of observers as the art pieces are chosen for display. In truth, everyone wants the audience to like and possibly purchase the product directly, in ticket sales, or both.

Back in 1994, I was teaching a course in the Africana Studies Department at Brooklyn College called "The Black Family." I was very glad to show my students how our families survived the violent social stigma of racism in the United States because we cultivated the unique ability to adapt to life in the urban environment. I taught about the special role of our fathers, brothers, husbands, and sons who had a shorter life expectancy and difficulty protecting themselves and their families.

Another course I taught was "Black Women in America," and among the many roles I considered to be profound was the role of women as national organizers. As early as the 1890s, they put their children in a wagon drawn by a horse, suckled babies at their breasts and rode through town and country, organizing women to attend annual state and national conventions to address the social needs of families and communities. With the addition of invited community speakers, my students presented creative vignettes in a workshop combining both classes called "The Black Family: Alternatives for Survival."

Well, nothing happens all by itself in a vacuum. At the same time these positive activities took place on campus, an art exhibit opened in November 1994 at the very sophisticated Whitney Museum of Art, formerly located on Fifth Avenue in Manhattan, called "The Black Male."

All I vividly remember were three sections of the exhibit. One depicted a boxing ring filled with rabbits in blackface. The two contenders, their assistants, and the referee were all adult rabbits with a bunch of little rabbits who looked like they were running around in a sorry, confusing mess. I don't recall seeing any female rabbits. Maybe they were all home pregnant, about to give birth to more rabbits. You see, rabbits are known to be highly reproductive. They have a lot of babies.

Then there was the European photographer Robert Mapplethorpe. He had a fascination with the phallus of men of Kemetic descent. At least a dozen black-and-white photographs of erect and partially erect phalluses were shown from different angles. Mapplethorpe created different shades in a film noir motif with dark shadows and light contrast peeking through a lens of flagellating fantasy, forgetting that it wasn't really his…or wishing it was…The Black Male. I wonder if he measured it to see if it was nine-and-a-half inches or more. This is all they really see. I'm not mad at him. I love the black phallus, too. That's just not all of the unique qualities of our men. In fact, they are multifaceted. The ones I know are virile, beautiful, talented, humorous, intellectual, educated, charming, loving, and strong individuals who want to provide for their families. That's what scares them most.

I recall the third section of the exhibit like it was yesterday. It made me do a double-take. Did I really see what I thought I saw? I took a breath, and there it was. A mantel. Some of us have a mantel in our homes, or we have visited homes with a mantel as the center of attention in the living room. It is usually decorated with special sculptures, maybe a set of candelabra or special family photographs. The mantel supports the structure of a real or imitation fireplace that emits warmth for the feet and comfort for the body on a cold winter night. Just thinking about this brings us to a cozy mental space.

This mantel was filled with trophies. It was crowded because everyone seemed to want his trophy in the exhibit, and the curator had to accommodate them all. The trophies were presented- assuming that all trophies are presented in a special ceremony -in honor of mostly New York Police Officers for killing a black man. Many of the trophies were molded in the shape of – guess what? You got it! A bunch of black phalluses. There must have been twenty-five or thirty on display. Many of the elaborate trophies were inscribed with erect phalluses and included the names of the Officers along with the dates of the killings. All kinds of guns filled in the spaces between the trophies. I had a good friend whose brother was killed by police in the 1960s in a case of mistaken identity, and his family has never been the same since then. I wondered if his phallus was in that number when the police came marching in.

I don't want to discuss the national controversy the exhibit stirred up because "The Black Male" was scheduled to tour the USA, including Los Angeles. I won't discuss in detail the quality of the other pieces or the profound works of seasoned, talented Kemetic American Artists who were excluded from the show. This exhibit goes deeper than that. Not having reviewed the exhibit prior, many teachers brought their classes to the exhibit, probably thinking that the Whitney Museum had more decorum than that. The Kemetic woman who served as curator was probably a "front" for several racists who dictated the images and subliminal vignettes they wanted to engrave in the minds of the public as observers.

So, the minds of the attendees were reinforced in a truly subliminal, or not so subliminal way that Black Men breed like rabbits and fight each other in an environment that is a royal mess; their penises instill a mystique of love, fear, envy, and insecurity; they reward people who kill them off; and, as a result, whites are no longer threatened. In reality, the more the white police feel their own impotence, the quicker they will shoot.

Behaviors of white supremacists are the result of centuries of anti-Black beliefs that have been inculcated into the minds of their young, nurturing attitudes of disdain and arrogance that are acted out in overt aggression. The continuing patterns of police killing unarmed Kemetics and the resulting support of these behaviors by the criminal justice system are evidence of cultivated years of hatred.

Dr. Frances Cress-Welsing wrote about the white man's fear and fascination with the genetic material of the Black Man. She also presents an analogy of the pistol aimed forward as an extension of his erect penis among white men. We have been inundated in the media of TV and cinema with white men killing for perceived power since "lynching and cowboys and Indians." Ku Klux Klan perpetrators of the lynchings would cut the phalluses of the victims, dry them, and place them on their mantels as tokens of their heinous acts.

Another heinous killing took place in Minneapolis, Minnesota, on May 25, 2020, when 46-year-old George Floyd was held down on the ground by two officers while a third police officer held his knee at Floyd's neck for 8 minutes and 46 seconds, killing him due to asphyxiation. The incident resulted in simultaneous national and global marches and demonstrations supporting "Black Lives Matter." The incident videotaped George Floyd repeatedly saying, "I can't breathe," on the cell phone of a 17-year-old female who witnessed the incident.

In reality, do police killers of sons of Kemet go home and "jerk off"? Does the mere mental recall of a Brother's killing help them get their nature to rise? Do they have nightmares of being chased by a big black phallus or loving dreamscapes of being entered by one? Only their shrinks know for sure. These deep-seated psychological defense mechanisms cannot be resolved with superficial training and body cameras.

When viewed through a wider lens, these seemingly random, rapid succession killings of unarmed Kemetic men, women, and children appear to be taking place under a higher directive. These acts of violence appear in an ebb and flow of non-stop massacres and lynchings from the Civil War/Reconstruction to the present. The issue again arises in Chapter 6: "Life in Our Father's House" and social impacts on family stability, economic security, and disenfranchisement.

Solutions Specialists must become aware of a strategy I call "set-up," which:

- Perpetuates nationwide random demonstrations so that we are blind to or distracted from what is really going on; and/or
- Stirs up the emotion of anger, instigating random retaliation enough to initiate an emergency "state of civil conflict."

We are deeply saddened for the individuals whose lives were taken, and sincere condolences are sent to every family. We are compelled to convert negative emotions of anger into positive actions. Key activities would take us away from the streets and into places and safe spaces for "Meet-Ups." We would then develop and implement ongoing rapid-cycle change strategies designed to Save-Our-Selves.

Today, District Attorneys choose Grand Jurors in secrecy to actuate an orgy with hand-picked witnesses with protected identities who present rubber-stamped sworn testimonies and pre-approved signed affidavits approved by police chiefs, ejaculating in roller-coaster orgasms supporting decisions of no indictments under the hooded protection of the law.

That scenario is deep, but then, I wonder about the meaning of the same pistol when Black men kill each other. Is it merely animal and territorial? Have some of our men not learned to handle their emotions? Do they believe that it is "punking out" to experience peaceful conflict resolution? Do they need to kill each other to protect their drug "turfs" as they continue to poison our people with a drug dependency, resulting in their inevitable arrest, incarceration, or death? Do the police think in their heads, "Go on and kill them – they are killing each other anyway?" Do other people think, "Go on and say the "n-word" because they call each other the "n-word" anyway? This is an in-house challenge for us to address.

Amidst the national and international media explosion around "I Can't Breathe!" "Hands up! Don't Shoot!" within the "Black Lives Matter Movement," Former New York Mayor DiBlasio was highly criticized by other politicians when he admitted having a "talk" with his biracial teenage son. You better believe I had a "talk" with my son when he was that age. I cautioned him to be careful in his every move.

I told him how to behave in the presence of the police. To say "Yes Sir" and "No Sir" and be unemotional and polite in their presence.

In my deep radicalness, I even told him to stand back if the police were assaulting me, his Mother. He answered that he didn't think he could do that. I emphatically told him that he better because both of us would be locked up, and he definitely couldn't help me then. He knew early on that his enemies were three-fold – other white people, the police, and his peers. He had to have his mental and physical defenses up among other Kemetic teens and against peer group pressure leading to drug use, violence, death, or incarceration.

As a City Research Scientist, one of my tasks was to manage several teams of individuals who conducted HIV prevention interventions for recently released and incarcerated individuals at the jail on New York City's Riker's Island. This city jail daily housed more than 20,000 inmates in each of nine facilities at that time, mostly Kemetic-American and Hispanic men and women. One of the facilities housed gay inmates, another housed women, including babies under 12 months old, another high security, others general populations, and a medical center with isolated housing for tuberculosis-infected individuals.

I had an opportunity to witness firsthand and take a deeper look into understanding this reality. Some inmates whose families could produce bail were detained briefly and released. Some were waiting as long as a year to go to Court and see a Judge. Some completed their sentencing and were waiting to be transferred to an upstate long-term prison facility.

Statistics are important in the eyes of evaluators. This is how we see the world. We can't help this. It's a part of our nature. As social research scientists, we are trained to be very objective and not react emotionally. These are just numbers.

So, I raised my eyebrows a little when I discovered a fact that forever changed my thinking. Roughly 87 % of the individuals in prison upstate came from only seven zip codes in New York City from a citywide total of 1,752 zip codes. They came from East and West Harlem, South Bronx, Bedford-Stuyvesant, Brownsville, East New York, Bushwick in Brooklyn and South Jamaica in Queens. All of them were in custody, receiving "three hots and a cot." In lay terms, three hot meals and a place to sleep.

Geographically, huge areas of the seven zip codes in New York City have become so gentrified that it resulted in the decrease in arrest and imprisonment of Kemetic residents to feed into the New York State prison system. This also partly results in an unprecedented reduction in violent crime in general. Paroles have been denied, and incarcerations have been extended to maintain population counts in the facilities. This may also apply to other cities and states throughout the United States.

> "But the forces that drove the Great American Crime Decline remain a mystery. Theories abound among sociologists, economists, and political scientists about the causes, with some hypotheses stronger than others. But there's no real consensus among scholars about what caused one of the largest social shifts in modern American history." (Ford: 2016)

I will momentarily take readers off on a Spiritual Tangent and explain my theory with support on the catalyst that influenced the residual social effects that brought about the "Great American Crime Decline."

It all began with "Ori Activation" (the closest translation of Ori is the Soul) during the first "Million Man March." The March was conceived by Minister Louis Farrakhan, Leader of the Nation of Islam and executed by the Fruit of Islam on October 16, 1995.

Minister Farrakhan gave power to the prayers for forgiveness and atonement preceding the massive physical embrace that took place during the event. "Ori" is a precious, subtle, ancient Yoruba reality that predates Western Religious thought and practice by more than 12,000 years. I'm sharing this to illustrate the ability we have as a people to collectively manifest our individual, family, and community well-being to continue executing positive change in our lives.

In 2004, S. Levitt wrote in the Journal of Economic Perspectives 18 (1), "Understanding why crime fell in the 1990s: Four factors that explain the decline and six that did not." He concluded from his analysis that "the simplistic accounts of why crime fell offered by so-called experts to the media can be quite misleading."

Most recently, in *The New York Times: Morning*, August 8, 2022, G. Lopez presents a graph showing evidence of this downward trend in violent crime since 1995. (See Table 1: Annual Murder Rates in the U.S.)

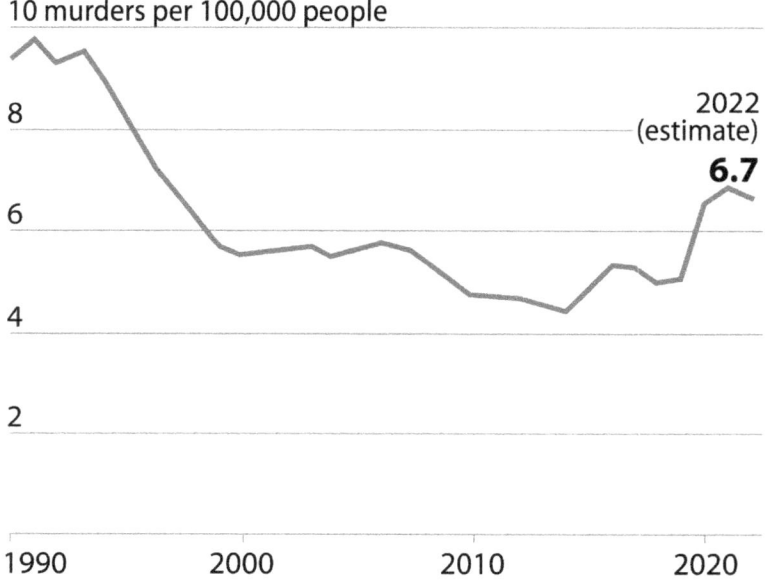
**Annual murder rates in the U.S.**

I contend that the "*Ori Activation*" during the **Million Man March** and its "**Power of Atonement**" resulted in immediate short- and long-term individual, family, and community effects as a result of the million-plus mass treatments to the "*Ori*" for those present.

Atonement is defined as "reconciliation after enmity or controversy." Minister Farrakhan spoke about the power of forgiveness and encouraged the million men to ask each other for forgiveness and embrace one another. Forgiveness and atonement are aspects of *ori* development. *Ori* is about one's Soul and relationship to God and the Universe. "Consciousness of one's ori allows personal control of negativity in order to know and fulfill one's destiny. Hate, jealousy, fear, and envy are some of the negative emotions that prevent ori cultivation." (2018) *Ifa: Path to Enlightenment*. Baba Ade Ifaleri Olayinka.

At least another million witnessed the same on live television. This is fascinating in and of itself and even more revealing regarding the social science of it all.

Not to get too technical, this represents a cost-effective analysis for the vast majority of our people, which caused the nationwide increase of Quality-Adjusted-Life-Years (QALYs–pronounced: qualies) for the 28 years since 1995. Life itself continues to be a major benefit – fewer thousands killed and fewer thousands incarcerated; decrease in populating the public and private prisons; decrease in inmates providing free labor; increase in mothers and fathers providing for families; increase in those receiving higher education degrees and other training; another generation of families thrive; and an increase of people gainfully employed for self or other employers.

Statistical data is available for each of these examples. Remember, this decline in violent crime is considered "one of the largest social shifts in modern American history." QALYs are measured based on a given intervention for a specific disease in a program to justify allocating resources for additional services.

"QALYs are measures of longevity, in units of years of life, adjusted for the 'quality' of life during those years. By translating health outcomes into time-based units, each is equivalent to one perfectly healthy year of life. QALYs allow the combination of information on both survivorship and the experience of health during the surviving years" Joshua A. Salomon, *International Encyclopedia of Public Health, 2nd Ed.* (2017).

Just imagine one patient in one medical program who receives an intervention and is healthy for one year equals one QALY. Now consider *Ori Activation* as a mental health intervention for 2,000,000 individuals, the impact of which was felt for 27 years (even allowing for deaths due to various causes and, despite other stressful Social and Structural Determinants of Health), the exponential results of 54,000,000 QALY's from this special treatment attest to the resilience of our people and our ability to adapt and thrive. The numbers due to *Ori Activation* are immeasurable as a priceless value for lives well-lived.

The Social Determinants of Health include, but are not limited to, quality jobs, economics, quality education, access to quality health care, neighborhood stability, and social and community context (go to: https://health.gov › healthypeople).

The Structural Determinants of Health include blocks to our well-being – racism, sexism, public and social policies, societal and cultural values, etc.)[6]

At any rate, I publicly and sincerely thank Allah, Olodumare, and God Almighty for giving Minister Farrakhan the divine inspiration to save so many lives in so many different ways and the Fruit of Islam for carrying out the plan. Ase-O!

Before discovering the imprisonment by zip code statistics, I learned another piece to this puzzle impacting youth development. It was the story of The Woodlawn Organization (TWO) in the inner city of Chicago around 1972. Long story short, two major gangs were competing for turf, killing each other, and wreaking havoc in the Woodlawn area. Clergy members got the gang leaders together and convinced them to work in unison for youth development. They formed TWO and began making significant changes in the community initiated by the youth. They applied for and received a Federal Grant to support their mission at that time.

Now, here's the hitch–the local Social Workers Union complained that they no longer had clients to counsel and petitioned against the Federal Government that all Federal funding for programs first had to be approved locally before receiving support. The key here is that mostly white Social Workers were threatened about losing their jobs because they had no clients who required their services.

---

6      HIMSS. (2021, May 13). Social Determinants of Health. https://www.himss.org/resources/social-determinants-health

Mr. Brazier, President of TWO, had this to say:

"The project was killed because the political establishment could not tolerate an independent organization such as TWO receiving Federal funds controlled by the establishment itself. The project was killed because white society refused to permit indigenous leaders in the black ghetto to deal with problems of alienated youth– a problem that white society, by its indifference and racism, has forced on the ghetto."

I recently viewed a program hosted by Gil Noble, former NBC TV Host of "Like It Is," which originally aired in 1990. Mr. Noble interviewed a former CIA Agent who felt the need to "come out" and expose his work during the Black Power Movement. He revealed that he provoked anger and hostility between opposing factions in California, facilitated an opportunity for them to "acquire" weapons from an "unguarded" arsenal, and "set-up" the scene where young Kemetic Brothers were killing each other.

Could it be in other cities right now that a situation of "setup" is impacting Kemetic males causing them to kill each other? Can these killings be brought about by provocative agents who:

- Provoke their emotions
- Create angst between factions
- Make guns accessible to "warring" factions
- Cause youth to kill each other and innocent bystanders

In another personal experience, around 1988, I was director of two youth programs in downtown Brooklyn: School to Employment and Structured Education Support Program. I visited George Wingate High School in Crown Heights to recruit participants. The halls were filthy with piles of trash that were never picked up. Students were milling around the hall and hanging around the cafeteria in a cacophony of noise from voices and boom-boxes. During that visit, I could not access anyone of authority, and I left shaking my head.

Community Leaders in another part of Brooklyn, Ft. Green, Clinton Hill, and Bedford Stuyvesant, were meeting to form a Youth Coalition. My Executive Director advised me that I should not attend this meeting. It didn't make sense to me as I was still recruiting participants for our programs. I was charged with insubordination because I attended the meeting. Much later, I realized that the youth in Central Brooklyn, for whom we attempted to intervene, were targeted to kill each other or feed into Rikers and the upstate prison system. Supporting the conspired plan for local gentrification, politicians were selling our youth "down the river" (now we say throwing them "under the bus"). The program I worked for was supported by a local politician.

In retrospect, this continues to take place. Productive men made decisions that caused our children to be psychologically separated from their families. Parents accepted school integration following the social and economic protests of the late sixties and early seventies, allowing the "system" to control the development of our children attending public schools.

Three key events took place in 1968 and were introduced into the African-American community. They were drug proliferation, special education designation, which included major bureaucratic changes in the entire education system from curriculum to administrative supervision, and the invention of the human immunodeficiency virus (HIV), which causes AIDS. Imagine how many human services jobs we have been providing for others to feed their families.

Similarly, the parent-teacher community control conflicts that emerged out of I.S. 271 in Ocean Hill-Brownsville, Brooklyn and I.S. 201 in East Harlem between 1968 and 1972 failed the community because they could not eliminate poorly functioning teachers. In New York State, the Teachers Union and National Education Association (NEA) are in major conflict with Governor Andrew M. Cuomo regarding the issue of effective teaching and learning. Again, the issue following 45 years of damage remains -

Union support of ineffective teachers. A chain is only as strong as its weakest link. The United States is far behind other countries in Science, Technology, Engineering, and Mathematics (STEM) training and development.

For this reason, our people become victims of poor and failing education. What are we doing to Our-Selves and each other? Let us not continue to be stuck on social media following marches with no direction and no personal or family plan or strategy to get out of this collective mess! Are we too complacent or afraid to step out of the box? Our very survival depends on a new way of being for us all!

Kemetic Americans and Hispanic people of color are being raised like cattle, victims of poor and failing education, cultivated to provide very low, almost free labor into the prison industrial complex. In the year 2000, the prison force of more than 2,000,000 individuals nationwide and the products they manufactured or services they provided were not defined or transparently identified as they relate to the Gross Domestic Product or Gross National Product.

Let us look at what Harold Cruse meant when he was quoted in the Introduction that we synthesize "Black social data which has already accumulated." According to the Bureau of Justice Statistics (Beck & Harrison 2001), "Overall, the U.S. incarcerated 2,071,686 persons at year-end 2000." (That is two million, seventy-one thousand, six hundred eighty-six, mostly people of color.)

Since then, there has been an unexplainable drastic reduction in crime and incarceration, which has been mysteriously termed the "Great American Crime Decline (mentioned previously), which caused one of the largest social shifts in modern American history" (Ford 2016). By year-end 2019, the total prison population was 1,430,800. "The imprisonment rate in 2019 was lowest since 1995" (Carson, 9).

We need to change the narrative associated with descendants of Kemet and the levels of fear and safety in the inner city. The large financial investments put into constructing private jails and prisons have resulted in a nationwide negative return on their investment. State and Federal prison and jail facilities have generally become underpopulated, and many have closed.

Let us re-examine the reality of fear. We are familiar with life the way it is. We know it is getting worse for us. Life is harder for others, too. Let us focus on Self, and as Malcolm says, "Let's go back into the closet – then come out swinging." Begin with self as we re-examine a week of activity. Number one: Turn off the television, video games, and handheld media distractions. Use that time just to think. There are many concerns; just begin with the most pressing. Where can we as individuals put special effort into changing just one aspect of our lives?

Caught up in Baby Daddy, Baby Mama Drama? This serves as a smoke screen. Best Friend, Worst Enemy? Let it go. There is serious stuff going on. Religion? I am this, and you are that– so you must believe exactly what I believe, or we cannot get along. We cannot allow ourselves to fall into this superficial snare of divisiveness. Choose issues that affect us all, and commit to act on them together.

Drug use? Low-level users are detained as we speak. Not the way! Synthetic marijuana, also called "Spice" or "K-2," is beginning to proliferate to further immobilize another generation of our youth as an updated flavor of chemical warfare. We must become more sophisticated than falling into a trap like that.

It's important to note that just because authorities say the law changed and now it's legal doesn't mean it's all right for you. I am speaking about recreational marijuana use. Individuals should critically assess their inclination to physically awaken earlier or stay up late, fulfilling commitments to make changes in our communities. Were you able to arrive at solutions and carry them out with other "420" users before the full legalization of recreational cannabis?

"In order to make informed decisions about whether cannabis is right for you, it's important to understand its active ingredients and how they activate the body and brain." It is Your / Our Prerogative - S-O-S – "We Save-Our- Selves…!"

I invite you to visit the Good RX website for specific details about the following points concerning the adverse side effects of recreational marijuana use:

- Cannabis plants that produce mind-altering effects are typically high in THC, and cannabis plants with high CBD (and little or no THC) are legally defined as hemp.
- THC's effects are mostly due to binding at the CB1 receptor, which is found in many brain regions involved in thinking, planning, pain, bodily movements, learning and emotions.
- Cannabis can impact one's coordination and thinking, and these impairments could negatively impact work or school performance.
- Certain vulnerable populations should be wary of cannabis or avoid it altogether.
- Decades of research have shown that cannabis interferes with brain development, and teenagers should wait to use cannabis until at least age 21.
- Cannabis use at an early age has also been linked with an increased risk for psychosis and other mental health problems and can also make symptoms of bipolar disorder worse[7].

www.goodrx.com/wellbeing/substanceuse/ risks-benefits-of-legal-marijuana#real-risks

It is time for us to pay attention to our own health in order to Save-Our-Selves (S-O-S). I learned a poem in Mr. Sealy's fifth-grade class at P.S. 36 Queens. It always stuck with me, and I have counseled people with it over the years:

---

7     Hall, W., & Degenhardt, L. (2008). Cannabis Use and the Risk of Psychotic Disorders. World Psychiatry, 7(2), 68–71. https://www.ncbi.nlm.nih.gov/pmc/articles/PMC2424288/

### "It's All in the State of Mind"

If you think you are beaten, you are,
If you think you dare not, you don't,
If you like to win, but you think you can't,
It's almost a "cinch" you won't.

If you think you'll lose, you've lost,
For out in the world, you find
Success begins with a person's will;
It's all in the state of mind.

Full many a race is lost
Ere ever a step is run;
And many cowards fail
Ere ever their work's begun.

Think big and your deeds will grow,
Think small and you'll fall behind,
Think that you can and you will;
It's all in the state of mind.

If you think you're outclassed, you are,
You've got to think high to rise,
You've got to be sure of yourself before
You can ever win a prize.

Life's battles don't always go
To the stronger or faster woman or man
But sooner or later the ones who win,
Are the people who think they can.[8]"

---

8    Wintle, W. D. (1905). Thinking. Retrieved from https://allpoetry.com/poem/8624439-Thinking-by-Walter-D-Wintle

# SOURCES

*The Isis papers: The keys to the colors*
Cress-Welsing, M.D., F. (1991). Third World Press: Chicago.

*Black Power/ White Control*
Fish, J.H. (1973). Princeton University Press: Princeton, New Jersey.

*"What caused the great crime rate decline in the U.S.?"*
Ford, M. (2016, April 15). The Atlantic. Retrieved from: https://www.theatlantic.com/politics/archive/2016/04/what-caused-the-crime-decline/477408/

*"Understanding why crime fell in the 1990's"*
Levitt, S. (2004). Journal of Economic Perspectives. 18(1)

*"Annual Murder Rates in the U.S."*
Lopez, G. (August 8, 2022). New York Times: Morning.

*Ifa: Path to enlightenment*
Olayinka, A. I. Olayinka, V. H. Ed. (2018) CCGR Publishing, New York City.

*"Toward a theory of community development."*
Harris, V.L. (1982). Unpublished

*"Prisoners in 2000,"*
Beck, A.J., Ph.D. & Harrison, P.M. (2001, August). Bureau of Justice Statistics Bulletin, NCJ 188207 (p. 1)

*"Prisoners in 2019,"*
Carson, E.A. Ph.D. (2020, October). Bureau of Justice Statistics Bulletin, NCJ 255115 (p. 1,9)

# CHAPTER THREE

*Saggin': Beyond Blaming the Victim*

## Highlights:

- Fifty-six years ago, in 1967, Harold Cruse directed our attention to respond to the plight of our "Lost Black Generation" alienated in the Urban Black Cities.
- Forty-one years ago, in 1982, Jawanza Kunjufu expressed the need to "Counter the Conspiracy to Destroy Black Boys" and continued for at least ten years to outline strategic objectives for families, communities, and educators to achieve this goal.
- Thirty-three years ago, in 1990, Dr. Amos Wilson observed the social-psychological reality of Black-on-Black Crime, which led to his critical analysis of the "psychodynamics of Black self-annihilation in service of white domination."
- Descendants of Great Kemet! S- O-S We Must Save-Our-Sons. Let's Get It On!

"Today we have a Lost Black Generation—very young and very historically conditioned. They are lost within the deep canyons of the urban cities, aliens to the white Western culture of the American style, whose exile is within themselves. Their alienation is reflected in many ways—in delinquency, crime, sex, drugs, hatred of whites, sometimes in hatred of themselves, and sometimes even in poetry and other art forms. These outlets become their method of self-exile within a social system from which there is no longer any escape…" (Cruse, 533)

Jawanza Kunjufu continued this conversation 40 years ago, in 1982, in his first book in a series of ten, *Countering the Conspiracy to*

*Destroy Black Boys*, where he defines conspiracy as an act of plotting together to harm someone. He describes this conspiracy as complex and interwoven, with obvious and less obvious contributors to these acts.

"Those people who adhere to the doctrine of white racism, imperialism, and white male supremacy are easier to recognize. Those people who actively promote drugs and gang violence are active conspirators…What makes the conspiracy more complex are those people who, through their indifference, perpetuate it as parents, educators, and white liberals who deny being racists, but through their silence allow institutional racism to continue" (Kunjufu, 1).

Kunjufu explored various themes in the attempt to educate and influence sons of Kemet by writing books such as *Motivating and Preparing Black Youth to Succeed, Developing Positive Self-Images, Lessons from Black History, To Be Popular or Smart: The Black Peer Group, Black Economics: Solutions for Economic and Community Empowerment,* and (1992) *Hip Hop vs. MAAT: A Psycho/Social analysis of Values.*

He suggested we address values related to male responsibility, gun control, and job acquisition to deter gang formation. He mentioned that illegal drugs were more available in jail than on the streets and that prosecution for low-level possession of drugs disproportionately fell on Kemetic youth rather than white youth.

Thirty-two years ago, in 1990, Dr. Amos Wilson, PhD, psychologically analyzed Kemetic youth who commit violent crimes against their peers. *Black-On-Black Violence* refers to the assaultive, homicidal, and suicidal violence committed by Blacks against Blacks in ways that are self- and mutually- destructive, egregious (blatant), and gratuitous (unjustified)." In what he called the psychodynamics of Black self-annihilation in service of white domination, Wilson shows us how white Americans present themselves as victims of street crime when, in truth, they are far less likely to personally experience an act of street crime than Kemetic individuals.

However, in my opinion, media over-exposure to crime in fiction and newscasts may enhance their insecurity and embed in the white psyche the justification for a "war on crime" and the so-called "war on drugs," which tends to be directed against those of Kemetic descent.

Wilson states, "Whites create within and among themselves external conflicts, self-incriminations, and tensions." From my observation of white people, I have often reminded myself that they are not nice to each other, so how can I expect whites to be nice to me or my people?

"The white community makes it appear that it is threatened by a menacing Black community; an evil, criminal Black community which jeopardizes its existence; not the evil criminal inclinations it contains within its own bosom…" thus by compulsively defending itself against the "projected threat" the Black community represents, the white community defends itself against its own self-generated, but self-denied, threats. Wilson resolves another key to this puzzle when he concludes that the white community becomes blind to its own negative characteristics and the positive characteristics of its scapegoat, the Black community (Wilson, 64).

Wilson continues to psychoanalyze the black-on-black perpetrators of crimes and the misplaced rationales resting deep in their minds that justify their "self-family-group" directed offenses without regret. He says the young Kemetic violators somehow believe this fear to be true, and they direct the white hatred projected at them back into the Kemetic community.

Syndicated columnist Leonard Pitts argued in 2014 that "the vast majority of violent crime is committed within– not between– racial groups. Crime is a matter of proximity and opportunity. People victimize their own rather than drive across town to victimize somebody else." Although this fact is true, the number of Kemetic American deaths due to firearm homicides remains staggering. *The Morbidity and Mortality Weekly Report*, October 7, 2022, states, "Non-Hispanic Black or African-American persons continued to experience the highest firearm homicide rates in every age group." Real numbers tell the story best.

See Table 2: Firearm Homicides by Age, Race, Ethnicity, United States 2021

**Table 2: firearm homicides by age, race, ethnicity, united states 2021**

Data for 2021 are provisional and as reported through August 7, 2022

| Age Group, Race, Ethnicity | Numbers | Rate Per 100,000 | Total Hispanic | **Total African American** | Total White |
|---|---|---|---|---|---|
| **Less Than 10 Years** | | | | | |
| Hispanic | 15 | 0.15 | 15 | | |
| African-American | 120 | 2.22 | | **120** | |
| White | 44 | 0.23 | | | 44 |
| **10 - 24 Years** | | | | | |
| Hispanic | 1,224 | 7.71 | 1,224 | | |
| African-American | 4,347 | 48.8 | | **4,347** | |
| White | 653 | 1.97 | | | 653 |
| **25 - 44 Years** | | | | | |
| Hispanic | 1,756 | 9.45 | 1,756 | | |
| African - American | 6,600 | 54.43 | | **6,600** | |
| White | 1,918 | 3.91 | | | 1,918 |
| **45 - 64 Years** | | | | | |
| Hispanic | 429 | 3.29 | 429 | | |
| African-American | 1,494 | 14.74 | | **1,494** | |
| White | 1,090 | 2.03 | | | 1,090 |
| **65 + Years** | | | | | |
| Hispanic | 37 | 0.73 | 37 | | |
| African-American | 164 | 3.11 | | **164** | |
| White | 357 | 0.85 | | | 357 |
| Sub-Totals | | | 3461 | **12,725** | 4062 |

Black/Kemetic-American people make up 13.5% of the total U.S. population. White people make up 75.8 % of the U.S. population. Native American/Alaskan Native comprise 1.3%. Together, we account for 90.6% of all Americans in this country. The combined remaining ethnic identities total 9.4%.

Kemetic Americans have a smaller population pool, so the damage from all deaths, including death due to firearm homicide, makes up an average death rate of 24.7%. Therefore, local Solution Specialists are challenged to decrease the incidence of homicide in our communities. A follow-up inquiry would be to determine what percentage of 12,725 firearm homicides of Kemetic-Americans in 2021 were attributed to local police shootings.

Amos Wilson presents psychoanalytic scenarios that support this contradiction throughout this book and the next (1992) *Understanding Black Adolescent Male Violence*. White criminologic capitalist profit-oriented America has many ulterior motives. It took me five decades of careful, focused study and observation to conclude that our sons are being nurtured and bred like animals to provide free labor to maximize profits within the prison industrial complex.

Low-level criminal drug use and/or sales justify long-term prison sentences, primarily for young Kemetic men. This prevents them from being nurturers and positive role models for their children and supporters of their wives or baby mamas.

Pregnant mothers using cocaine cause many of their female offspring to be sterile in a genocidal modus operandi to limit propagation. (See Chapter 4: Melanin Revisited.) Children born addicted to heroin and cocaine exhibit social and mental health behaviors that legally allow the early diagnosis and the dispensing of Prozac and Ritalin, maintaining distorted realities and dependency early in their lives.

School attendance in inner-city communities serves as a smokescreen to make it appear that a concerted effort is being made to facilitate opportunities for social advancement via public education. The tax base of inner-city schools in many cities has deteriorated so severely that the brick-and-mortar buildings have become vacated empty shells.

Our children's attendance in out-county, out-district areas justifies and generates federal, state, and local resources determined by population for those districts and communities. Inner-city neighborhoods no longer qualify for program funding because our children are bussed out to other areas. Urban-to-rural population shifts have directed increased Federal resource allocation and political representation away from the inner city.

Now, looking back so we can move forward, in 1997, The U.S. Commission on Crime recommended that state agencies develop local policies to suppress urban unrest while national Civil Rights and social unrest demonstrations were taking place. State and local police adopted a "Tough on Crime" agenda. This was spurred on by the media and politicians who supported rural prison town development projects. By the year 2000, almost 2,000,000 people of color were incarcerated or involved with the Criminal Justice System. However, the situation changed!

Between 1980 and 2000, prison town development took place under the assumption that crime and imprisonment would increase. The objective was to justify the establishment of private facilities with the intended profits from free labor supporting the Prison Industrial Complex.

As mentioned previously, violent crime has drastically decreased over the past 27 years since approximately 1995: "Violence started to rise in the 1960s and stayed at an extremely high level from the '70s to the beginning of the '90s. That's when violence started to fall. By 2014, the homicide rate was 4.5 per 100,000 people, the lowest rate in at least 50 years [1964 sic]. 2014 was really one of the safest years in the history of the U.S." (Florida, City Lab, 2018).

Inmate populations in jails and prisons have drastically decreased due to the massive reduction in homicides and violent crime. There is a need to change the false narrative regarding inner city crime among people of color, the fear aroused by isolated news events, and more than twenty years of fictitious TV media episodes.

In my discussions about sagging pants, I heard through the grapevine that Kemetic men wore low-hanging, unbelted pants during the period of enslavement. They were not allowed to belt or tie up their pants because this would keep them from running far or fast in escape attempts. Other more popular origins emerged from the prison experience where young men would walk around in the facility letting others know that they were "claimed" by someone else as lovers, so their status was "hands off" to other inmates. Possibly, belts less than two inches and shoelaces were considered contraband to prevent potential suicides.

I became personally cautious of "blaming the victim," instead preferring for them to make a statement about themselves. At different times, I have heard people say, "Why doesn't he just pick up his pants?" "I don't want to see his butt hanging out." "I am offended!" "I saw a guy running, trying to catch a bus. He looked ridiculous running like that."

A saggin' person is so busy holding up his pants that he can't hold his groceries or books. Others have cautioned that we as adults have a responsibility not to speak our individual opinions about saggin'. It would empower them as younger and older adults to decide for themselves and actualize a change in the self-image they want to project to the world.

Jawanza Kunjufu would probably say it had to do with a lack of values when a person exposes his private parts to the public, including elders, women, young boys and girls. Amos Wilson would probably attribute saggin' to a psychological need to insult and degrade others since he was insulted and degraded by them. I would begin by not blaming them for the image they are projecting. Society has dealt them a rough hand. We have had 50 years of discussions about our youth in crisis. We need to change this reality or experience 50 more years of the same if we are blessed to live that long.

They are making a non-verbal statement about the social state of affairs or dead end we are experiencing. I see a person who is depressed, nameless, stressed, and faceless, showing that he is strong and powerful because he can do what he wants with his body. He wants to insult others because he turns and gazes to see the reactions of those who see him. Not saying, "Look what you've done to me!" But instead, "I don't care."

Deep down, he really cares, or he wouldn't be "shouting" so loud. If he sees it as just a style, then I look forward to the evolution of a style and image invoking self-activation and self-actualization. Hey, my young—and older- Kemetic Brothers! It becomes your prerogative! Ultimately, it's up to you. Stop and Think!

## The Economics of Black Urban Expression

The economic irony of the urban expression of our youth is its global influence. The world embraces the popular culture of our youth. The urban speech in rap and hip-hop with its rhythmic vocalizations, urban break-dancing– however dated it might be, urban fashions, and urban cinema. There is a global economic source for our cultural output. Let us put our heads together and discover, plan, and strategize ways to maximize profits from our creative expression to benefit our communities. Let us collectively activate and continually perpetuate our mission to Save-Our-Selves.

In New York City, in August 2023, nationwide and globally, we celebrated 50 years of Hip Hop. Venues large and small, a Concert at Yankee Stadium, the Apollo Theater, block parties, and underground graffiti are accepted as a mainstream art form. Break dancing became a competitive style of movement to the rhythms. This is a fantastic update from my first edition.

Back in the day, mainstream music producers never accepted hip-hop, so they went rogue, spinning their own sounds, producing their own beats, marketing their creative output, funding their own concerts, building the genre into global performances enjoyed by millions, and making millions.

*Saggin': Beyond Blaming the Victim*

The stars have been giving back to the communities in many creative philanthropic ways. *The Grio* website and podcast tell how the artists are "using their success to lift up their communities and beyond" in the article "10 World Hip-hop Stars Who are Giving Back." One-by-One and All-Together – Yes We Can!

 https://thegrio.com/2023/05/05/ten-world-hip-hop-stars-giving-back/https://thegrio.com/2023/05/05/ten-world-hip-hop-stars-giving-back/

# SOURCES

*The Crisis of the Negro Intellectual*
Cruse, Harold. (1967). William Morrow & Company: New York. p. 533.

*Countering the Conspiracy to Destroy Black Boys.*
Kunjufu, Jawanza. (1985). African American Images: Chicago. p. 1

*Black-on-black violence: The psychodynamics of black self-annihilation in service of white domination.*
Wilson, Amos, N. (1990). AfrikanWorld Infosystems: New York. 31-32

*Understanding black adolescent male violence: Its remediation and prevention.*
Wilson, Amos, N. (1992). Afrikan World Infosystems: New York.

Florida, R. (2018, January 16). *The Great Crime Decline and the Comeback of Cities.* City Lab. Retrieved from The Great Crime Decline and the Comeback of Cities, Patrick Sharkey: https://www.bloomberg.com/news/articles/2018-01-16/understanding-the-great-crime-decline-in-u-s-cities

Pitts, Leonard. (2014) Was originally quoted in the Albuquerque Journal, but this publication removed the article by Mr. Pitts entitled: Crime is a Matter of Proximity and Opportunity, not Race.

(NBC News article: Small Towns Used to See Prisons as a Boon. Now, Many Don't Want Them. https://www.nbcnews.com/news/us-news/small-towns-used-see-prisons-boon-now-many-don-t-n1270147

# CHAPTER FOUR

*Melanin Revisited*

## Highlights:

- Let us take a deeper look at ourselves.
- Why are *we* so unique?
- What makes *us* the objects of continued institutional disenfranchisement in the face of our true contribution to World Development?
- We can use our God-given attributes to improve our individual and community well-being.
- Once we become consciously aware of the melanin in our bodies, we can enhance our ability to re-examine our options.
- We can use what we have to reinforce our source and power in manifesting projects for change to bring about collective transformation.

In his groundbreaking book, *The Souls of Black Folks*, W.E.B. DuBois said in 1907 that the "problem of the 20th Century would be the problem of the color line." We are 23 years into the 21st Century, and globally, economic and social barriers and opportunities continue to be drawn around skin color. Decisions in high places are determined based on racial and ethnic categories of good, better, and best.

One hundred years ago, in 1915, Alain Locke, possibly the earliest Kemetic-American philosopher, examined cultural differences, cultural democracy, and cultural contacts and wrote with perplexing wonder that white people would make critical decisions based on race, even if the choice were detrimental to themselves as a people.

"Sometimes a region such as the South, or a class such as white workers, acted against its own economic interests in a seemingly blind attempt to maintain a benighted racial superiority. The question was not whether racism was a trick played by capitalists on the working classes but why race was such a divisive tactic. Such feelings spread and infected the entire group when it felt its collective survival threatened." (1992, Stewart, J. C.)

The varying skin tones, hair textures, and facial characteristics make us unique as individuals– not bad, just different from the European model. What do we of Kemetic descent have that makes us different? Why do we seem to appear to whites as a social psychological threat?

Let us examine this in another way. Let us remove ourselves from the deprivation conversation. Our history in the United States gives us countless examples of scientific discoveries, patented inventions, "assisted" patented inventions, superior problem resolutions, art and musical output, and achievements in sports and dance. Lewis Latimer was credited for "assisting" Thomas Edison with his experiments on electricity.

How many books, screenplays, reports, and proposals have we written that were copied, adopted and implemented by others without credit or compensation to us? We innovate, and they imitate. We know we can, and we do. Let us look more deeply into what we have that *they* do not have– concentrations of melanin in different parts of our bodies in addition to skin and hair.

We see, hear, taste, smell, touch, and feel life via the melanin in our brains through liquid nerve cells that travel into the body. This gives us higher contact with the inner life of our emotions, spiritual, subconscious, sublime and extrasensory life. Synthetic drugs and negative emotional behaviors cause us to degrade our melanated powers. These drugs include cocaine, LSD, heroin, amphetamines, Ritalin, codeine, caffeine, mescaline, and processed and chemicalized junk foods.

These harmful chemicals bond to our melanin and become lodged throughout our bodies. "Black people with their higher melanin content are twice as addicted to synthetic drugs than other races. The drugs kill and have an effect on the mind, emotions, and the physical body of Black people—which means they act upon melanin" (Afrika, 10-11).

Melanin is a complex chemical compound that sends messages throughout the body to help regulate body functions. We are revisiting the many benefits and activities that will advance our ability to Save-Our-Selves. There is an associated liability due to the Vitamin D deficiency we experience the farther we are from the direct sunlight at the Equator. Vitamin D supplements may serve as a remedy to this reality. As always, check with your doctor first to confirm your supplement intake.

This chemical compound of melanin has its own unique structure within the human bodies of descendants of Kemet. The pinecone-shaped pineal gland, located in the middle of the brain, secretes melanin, which regulates all bodily functions and glands. Melanin molecules behave like powerful links locked together in a chain, allowing melanin to morph into many forms, vibrate with varying rhythms, and have the capacity to be flexible as the molecules seek to attract energy to themselves (Afrika, 7).

Western science classified races on Earth based on the melanin content inside the body and the skin. The Kemetic human body has the highest melanin content of all races, with millions, perhaps billions of melanin cells spread out and clustered together in key energy centers.

Melanin is efficient in capturing energy because its chemical structure will not allow any type of energy to escape once that energy has come into contact with its structure. Light waves and sound waves are both forms of energy. These energy particles and sound vibrations travel in space, where they contact the melanin structure in our skin and other areas of the body where the energy particles and sound vibrations are absorbed by melanin. "Melanin can rearrange its chemical structure to absorb all energy across the radiant energy spectrum" (Barnes, 18).

Melanin may be viewed as a battery that is partially charged and can always accept an additional charge. Our blessed God-given planet Earth provides this energy for free from the sun, thermal/radiant heat waves, cosmic rays/ultraviolet light, Earth's magnetic energy, electromagnetic energy, music and ultrasonic sound. Once the energy is stored inside the melanin battery, Kemetic individuals have a higher capacity for body metabolism and thinking ability.

The pineal gland is part of a system that enables us to learn new skills to improve our access to resources. Pineal glands of other ethnicities show different levels of calcification. Alcohol, addictive drugs, and junk food chemicals contribute to pineal calcification within the Kemetic body. Something that is calcified is hard, like teeth or bone. The healthy pineal gland within descendants of Kemet is vibrant and pulsating. Melanin is energized by sunlight that enters mainly from the eyes and skin. Melanin enables (King, 75) the flow of electrons in our bodies.

Melanin can alter consciousness by adapting to other social environments, hence the heightened ability to improvise (Afrika, 16-18). This is a characteristic of Black people's music, dance, acting, dress styles, hairstyles, language usage, inventions, science, art, and culture (Barnes, 55). Melanin functions for us every day of our lives in the following areas.

### Table 3: Melanin Enhances our Abilities

| 1 | Memory |
|---|---|
| 2 | Memory Retrieval |
| 3 | Intuition |
| 4 | Motivation |
| 5 | Movement (Motor Output) |
| 6 | Sensory Output |
| 7 | Feeling Sensations |
| 8 | Emotions |
| 9 | Utilizing External Energy Sources (Light, Sound) |
| 10 | Anti (Skin) Cancer, For Most |
| 11 | High Morals |
| 12 | High Spirituality |
| 13 | Dreaming |

Carol Barnes goes on to say that we also see the world and experience it differently due to melanin's sedative and civilizing effects. He cautions that all these wonderful attributes can be altered and become toxic to the body if melanin is exposed to improper environments. For example, in our personal relationships, we hear half a story, and without investigating further, melanated people tend to overreact and jump to conclusions. This may result in accelerated disrespect and personal, family, and community conflict.

"Man is a microcosm in the sense of a tree in relation to a seed. Potentiality is the macrocosm since it includes all the possibilities of the tree. The seed will develop these possibilities, however only if it receives corresponding energies from our diets, the earth, and the sky. Man, who bears within him the total seed of the universe, including the seed of spiritual states, can identify with the totality and obtain nourishment from it."

"Man Know Thyself" was the fundamental principle of the

psychology of Kemet. George James observes, "Self-knowledge is the basis of all knowledge. The mysteries required as a first step, the mastery of the passions, which made room for the occupation of unlimited powers. What do we need to do to "master our emotions and cool our passions?" Dr. Richard King, M.D. (2010: 29)

Sometimes, it is important to put information together to arrive at critical conclusions that benefit us. In other words, we are putting two and two together. Given: the pineal gland is shaped like a tiny pinecone about the size of a pea, producing and generating melanin flowing out of its apex at the top point. Pinecones have certain features that we can use to help us transform how we see ourselves to change and transmute our worlds proactively. Transmutation involves changing from one nature, form, substance, or state into another. Positive visualization helps us to achieve goals individually. This type of transmutation is probably more effective if done collectively with others because so many different activities need to take place to change our state of becoming into a fresh state of being.

Now, back to the tiny little pinecone of a pineal gland fueled by the pituitary gland, manufacturing the melanin being pumped all over our bodies. In January 2015, MSN online featured an article written in the San Francisco Globe newspaper about a creator of sculptures, John Edmark, an inventor, designer, and artist who teaches design at Stanford University. He created printed sculptures "designed in such a way that the appendages or little tails that stick out match Fibonacci's Sequence, a mathematical pattern of numbers that manifest naturally in objects like sunflowers and pinecones.

When the sculptures are spun at just the right frequency, under a strobe light, a rather magical effect occurs: the sculpture seems animated or alive! The rotation speed is set to match with strobe flashes such that every time the sculpture rotates 137.5 degrees, there is one corresponding flash from the strobe."

The author at *SF Globe* goes on to say:

"What makes Fibonacci's Sequence so incredibly fascinating is that it manifests in nature in countless places, such as in the branching of trees, the arrangement of leaves on a stem, the flowering of baby broccoli, a nautilus shell, or even the spiral of galaxies; and that's just to name a few. One of the reasons that Fibonacci's Sequence appears in so many plants is because its particular arrangement of leaves along the stem allows for the most sunlight to hit each and every leaf. With its exposure to sunlight maximized, the plant then stands the best chance possible of properly photosynthesizing, growing stronger, and staying healthy."

The key here is that this arrangement allows for the most sunlight to hit each and every leaf. Let us act to our advantage and proactively, with full consciousness, using every particle of melanin in our bodies. This begins with sunlight. Sit in the sun or use reflected sunlight in our environment to generate health and healing. Focus on the conditions of melanin that function for us every day. This will help us to manifest our personal goals and objectives. We can stand "the best chance possible of properly photosynthesizing, growing stronger and staying healthy."

"What you see is not always the same as what is really happening. While Edmark's spinning sculptures create the illusion of the objects moving and morphing, the objects themselves are actually rigid forms and do not change in shape."

We can use our minds to consciously assist ourselves in changing our physical realities. "One-by-One and All-Together." Yes, We Can transform the challenging illusions we are experiencing and morph them into a new way of being. Of course, bringing about our new lives will take work and effort. We become motivated and enthusiastic, anticipating and assuring change when our mental space is no longer consumed with insults and deprivation conversations.

There are 12 Melanin Clusters in the body that are erroneously labeled chakras or meridians. Descendants of Kemet, or melanin-dominant people, have 12 clusters, and other races have fewer– they say seven. "The clusters can be stimulated by hand, bio-magnetics, and acupuncture needles. The stimulation can cause wellness and help with diseases" (Afrika, 57).

Sunlight energy passes through melanin superconductor doorways as a flow of electrons via donors or receptors throughout the holy black body melanin system. "The highest concentration of melanin in the body is at the root of each hair follicle." Dr. King shows how these magnetic fields work, for example, at the top of the spinal cord, which controls movement and rhythmic patterns, harmonics of sound waves, color, taste, and smell. "All of this is to say that a coil structure of African hair may be critical for magnetic field signal transduction of light and communication of the melanin transformed five sensory organs of the saved African soul" (King, 72).

Melanin is concentrated in the digestive system's gastrointestinal tract, vagina, uterus, penis, sperm storage sac, auditory nerves of the ears, retina and iris of the eyes, the spinal cord and the entire nervous system. The melanin absorbs synthetic drugs carried throughout the body, the cells readjust, and the toxic drugs lodge in different body areas. This causes potential long-term effects of liver damage due to drugs, soda, vinegar, and alcohol or kidney damage from consuming alcohol, processed sugars and table salt.

Another revealing fact about melanin and synthetic chemicals is the destruction of Kemetic descendant's female reproductive eggs. An adult woman who uses drugs can damage the eggs of her future daughter. Despite the ability of the adult woman's capacity to fight off the effects of drugs, marijuana, or alcohol, the fetus of the unborn baby girl, with the lifetime of all the eggs she will ever produce, will get high, lacking an immune system to resist the drugs. "The melanin in the eggs forms a bond with the drugs forming a type of mental, physical, and genetic alteration" (Afrika, 14).

Caucasians lack the genetic ability to produce significant levels of heavy molecular weight melanin called Eumelanin, which has its highest content in black people. (Afrika, 18) Black people with Eumelanin can manufacture and reproduce melanin by using sunlight, the amino acid tyrosine, the metal copper, and perhaps compounds like peroxides that use oxygen. The free radical use of oxygen allows it to break down toxic substances. Melanated people can use spirit and conscious awareness to mentally bring health and wellness to their spheres of influence.

The melanin researchers have given us special keys that help us to Save-Our-Selves. We are preparing physically, emotionally, and spiritually to take on certain tasks to help ourselves, our families and our communities to Save-Our-Selves. We can enhance this special melanin connection by cleansing our bodies of legal and illegal synthetic drugs. We can wean Our-Selves away from the over-consumption of junk foods. We can direct our minds to feel one another, visualize, listen, communicate and work together to arrive at creative solutions to our problems. Yes, We Can! Use sunlight and the Earth's magnetic energy to carry over apology messages and convey forgiveness, mutual trust, thankfulness, gratitude, and love.

*Let the transformation begin!*

I am reminded of the people in the movie *Avatar*, who surrounded their tree of life, held hands, connected with the land and collectively prayed to protect the planet from destruction by the invaders. Imagine the effectiveness of the work of a collective of pineal pinecones. One pineal cone with direct focus by meditating and drawing in the energy of the Sun can manifest active participation and positive change for an individual. We just have to begin with a spiritual cleansing so that we are of like mind and there is no "channel interference" or "channel noise" impacting the group process.

Before the digital age, channel noise came through as static when connecting to a particular radio or television station until you adjusted the knob and received a clear transmission. Channel interference also happens when riding in a car, and you are on the periphery of two different radio signals, so you hear two different conversations simultaneously. We want to prevent multiple thoughts from taking place as much as possible, so we work on clearing our minds of extraneous thoughts.

## Child Nurturing While Applying Melanin Consciousness

Child nurturing and development is the primary focus for family and community transformation. Beginning today, we can nurture children in a substance- and chemical-free environment. In 1991, Dr. Frances Cress-Welsing put out a charge reminding us of academic achievement using standards and codes of behavioral conduct in her seminal book, *The ISIS Papers: The Keys to the Colors*. She wrote these twenty-five years before the digital maneuvering of mind-probing attacks that embedded insults and infused male-female and ingroup confrontation, promulgating perpetual animosity among Kemetic Americans via so-called "reality show" interactions in the disguise of entertainment.

Dr. Cress-Welsing says that before age six, all Black children should be taught fundamental exercises in Black self-respect by following Black adult examples in the home, school, church, and neighborhood. In the case of teen parenting, Cress Welsing (250) admonishes us that "making a baby should no longer remain the criteria of Black manhood or womanhood for teenagers and should be determined solely on the basis of one's ability to be self-supporting and to function effectively under the pressures of white supremacy."

We should discuss these standards with those of like minds who are committed to bringing about change in our lives. It is truly a matter of personal choice to open our minds to achieve individual and community transformation. See Table 4: Black Self-Respect.

**Table 4: Black Self Respect**

| 1 | Stop name-calling one another. |
|---|---|
| 2 | Stop cursing at one another. |
| 3 | Stop squabbling with one another. |
| 4 | Stop gossiping about one another. |
| 5 | Stop snitching on one another. |
| 6 | Stop being discourteous and disrespectful towards one another. |
| 7 | Stop robbing one another. |
| 8 | Stop stealing from one another. |
| 9 | Stop fighting one another. |
| 10 | Stop using and selling drugs to one another. |
| 11 | Stop throwing trash and dirt on the streets and in places where Black people live, work and learn |

*The Four Agreements*, a Toltec wisdom book by author Don Miguel Ruiz, provides us with a practical guide to personal freedom. When reading and studying these agreements, we realize that Don Miguel Ruiz speaks universal truths to guide all communities.

The Toltecs, mentioned in Chapter 1, were a society of men and women of knowledge thousands of years ago in Southern Mexico. Young Toltecs were trained to incorporate the four agreements into their everyday life. These rules were there to prevent them from engaging in major misunderstandings amongst each other and to begin to recognize the "smoky mirror" of illusions presented by the wider society to keep them confused and block them from recognizing the real truth.

## BE IMPECCABLE WITH YOUR WORD

Speak with integrity. Say only what you mean. Avoid using the word to speak against yourself or to gossip about others. Use the power of your word in the direction of truth and love.

## DON'T TAKE ANYTHING PERSONALLY

Nothing others do is because of you. What others say and do is a projection of their own reality, their own dream. When you are immune to the opinions and actions of others, you won't be the victim of needless suffering.

## DON'T MAKE ASSUMPTIONS

Find the courage to ask questions and express what you really want. Communicate with others as clearly as you can to avoid misunderstandings, sadness, and drama. With just this one agreement, you can completely transform your life.

## ALWAYS DO YOUR BEST

Your best is going to change from moment to moment; it will be different when you are healthy as opposed to sick. Under any circumstance, simply do your best, and you will avoid self-judgment, self-abuse, and regret. (1997)

*"From the book The Four Agreements © 1997, Miguel Angel Ruiz, M.D. Reprinted by permission of Amber-Allen Publishing, Inc. San Rafael, CA www.amberallen.com All rights reserved. No electronic distribution."*

After laying the ground rules and experiencing this mental and spiritual cleansing, we are prepared for a Pineal Pinecone Circle. Everyone must have a pulsating pineal pinecone to participate. No one is being discriminatory. God created the qualifications. We can begin our groups with Fibonacci Sequence numbers: 1, 1, 2, 3, 5, 8, 13, 21, 34, 55, 89, ... Let's try this, working the Pulsating Pineal Pinecones!

Let us begin in small groups and define a peaceful space, preferably outside, to draw in the energy of the rising and setting, late day, comfortable any day Sun, or reflected sunlight from windows. Decide on a collective self, family, or community goal. Hold hands and feel the vibrational energies of one another. Sexual energies should not interfere, whether each setting is heterogeneous or homogeneous. Alternatively, cultivate self-control and maintain a platonic state of mind throughout this exercise. Collectively, each person forms a whole.

Members of organizations can work to plan and implement key objectives and change them once they are achieved. Be careful of individual channel noise of those with different intentions. Plan on other goals the next time you gather. Keep a record of successes or challenges, and "always do your best."

# SOURCES

*The souls of black folks.*
DuBois, W.E.B. (1907).

*Race contacts and interracial relations: Lectures on the theory and practice of race.*
Stewart, J.C., Ed. (1992) Locke, Alain LeRoy. (1915). Edited and with an introduction by Jeffrey C. Stewart. Howard University Press: Washington, D.C. 1992

*The power and science of Melanin: The biochemical that makes Black People Black.*
Afrika, Llaila. (2014). Holistic Therapies and Education Center: Indianapolis, Indiana.

*Melanin: The chemical key to black greatness.*
Barnes, Carol. (1988) C.B. Publishers: Houston, Texas

*Melanin: A key to freedom.*
King, Richard, M.D. (1995). U. B. & U. S. Communications Systems: Hampton, VA.

*African origin of biological psychiatry.*
King, R.D., MD. (2010, revised). Richard D. King: Los Angeles, California.

*The ISIS papers: The keys to the colors.*
Cress-Welsing, Frances. (1991). Third World Press: Chicago.

*The four agreements*
Ruiz, Don Miguel. (1997). Amber-Allen Publishing: San Rafael, California.

Lynch, E.D.W. (2015). Mesmerizing 3-D Sculptures That Appear to Animate When Spun Under A Strobe Light: https://laughingsquid.com/mesmerizing-3d-printed-sculptures-that-appear-to-animate-when-spun-under-a-strobe-light/

 http://artstyle.sfglobe.com/2015/01/14/3d-printed- sculptures-look-alive-when-spun-under-a-strobe-light/? src=share fb new 32233

# CHAPTER FIVE

*Ethnic Manipulation: A Case Study of Jamaica, Queens County, New York City*

We are witnessing the planned relocation of neighbors and replacement with different ethnic groups changing community cohesiveness and historical continuity:

- Supported by City Planning Departments and sanctioned by financial institutions – nationwide
- Assisted by drug dependence, manipulation of sons and daughters of Kemet
- Reinforced by the bureaucratic restructuring of the public education system to "dumb us down," negatively impacting job readiness
- Set the stage for major health disparities and HIV infection resulting in death and family disintegration
- Caused planned housing foreclosure of elders trying to "hold down the fort" as guardians of their grands and great-grands

This has brought about our critical mental health imperative for family and community cohesiveness.

I am a Queens girl.

Since 1955, my parent(s) owned and have lived in the same house for over 60 years in a small enclave in the town of St. Albans called Addisleigh Park. Queens is one of five Boroughs or counties that make up New York City. The Village of Jamaica hosts several towns: Jamaica Estates, Holliswood, Hollis, Cambria Heights, Ozone Park, South Ozone Park, Springfield Gardens, Rosedale, South Jamaica, and St. Albans.

In the early 1950s, ordinances were put in place in Addisleigh

Park, stating that certain owners were not allowed to sell their properties to people of Kemetic descent. Well, that did not last long. Eventually, many musicians, performers, doctors, dentists, educators, entrepreneurs, business owners, sports figures, and writers lived and worked in Addisleigh Park. Their names include Lena Horne, Count Basie, Brooke Benton, James Brown, W.E.B. DuBois, Roy Campanella, Joe Lewis and Illinois Jacquette, to name a few.

By 1960, I witnessed "white flight" when I was assigned to attend 7th and 8th grade at P.S. 134 in Hollis. School attendance went from mostly all white to mostly all Kemetic in two years. This was true for P.S. 147 in Cambria Heights. These eventually became feeder schools for the newly constructed I.S. 192 in Hollis. Students from 192 fed into Andrew Jackson High School, Cambria Heights. The saga of deteriorating education in this area did not occur in isolation and links to this travesty of manipulative injustice that is now being told.

Three of my four siblings and I became adolescents, and integration was in full swing. I attended Forest Hills High School in an exclusive Jewish area in Forest Hills, Queens. The swimming pool at the school was completely shut down to avoid multicultural access.

Two historical events during my high school years were the assassination of John F. Kennedy and the March on Washington in 1963. The New York City World's Fair at Flushing Meadow Park occurred in 1964. I experienced the events resulting from the assassination of Dr. Martin Luther King as a Freshman at Brooklyn College in 1968.

We were very much in tune with the activities of the Social and Economic Movements of the 1960s and 1970s. The older sister of my brother's good friend went to Mississippi on a Freedom Bus as a student at Queens College. My parents were involved in the "Sit-Ins" at the construction site to ensure the integration of new apartments at Rochdale Village. Our collective visions were far, and enthusiasm was high for future opportunities.

Then came heroin. Cocaine was not easily accessible yet. Mostly, the boys began using. Again, like day and night, things changed. The light had gone out for residents of Addisleigh Park. This story is true for many other towns and communities throughout the U.S. Most girls managed to attend and graduate from college. The boys, our future potential husbands and mates, fell by the wayside for the most part. This was the first wave of those who could acquire and maintain properties and legacies planted by our parents. The influx of drugs brought on distrust and individual isolation in the community.

My undergraduate college experience from 1968-1974 was characterized by student unrest, anti-Vietnam War, Civil Rights, and Black Power. There were demonstrations among Students for a Democratic Society (SDS), Brooklyn League of Afro-American Collegians (BLAC), SEEK Student's Association, and Puerto Rican Student's Association all over the campus. I was very active in a multicultural women's group, with the formation of the Brooklyn College Day Care Center for the mutual care of our young children while we attended class. The Day Care Center exists to this day, partnering with the College's Psychology and Education Departments.

Professors and students alike tried to make sense of these emotionally-charged social and political movements. While Kemetic-American and Puerto Rican-American students were involved in demonstrations, we noticed that many of the students from the Caribbean were attending class. Authorities also noticed this difference in behavior. There was no political solidarity about local issues. Their objective was to graduate from college. Eventually, the so-called African American college quota across the board began to be filled by students from Africa and those of Caribbean ancestry. I am not mad at them! This is just what happened.

Young Kemetic Americans had become the "sacrificial lambs" and were penalized for their roles in the social movements of the 1960s and 1970s. Eventually, local public high school education quality deteriorated throughout New York City. Andrew Jackson High School shut down by the time my two nephews were attending. The NYC Department of Education did not even wait to phase out new students gradually. By 1990, my family discovered that my son, as an electrical engineering major, was among only three Kemetic non-Caribbean students out of approximately 300 in the private college he attended in Upstate New York. On another note, college recruiters had begun quietly searching for Kemetic American descendant students to achieve that multicultural balance within their student bodies.

Along with education came opportunities for professional job availability. Openings came via placements in New York City agencies of Social Services, Health, and Education, just to name a few. Those with college degrees got hired. As recently as the late 1990s, under Mayor Giuliani, Kemetic Employees from the Caribbean and America began to be overlooked in favor of Bengalis from Bangladesh and Indians from India, who became employed in large numbers in the Department of Health and Mental Hygiene.

They were also hired as Indian and Bengali new teachers by the New York City Department of Education. Parents began complaining because their children could not understand the unfamiliar intonations and inflections in Bengali and Indian voices. This impacted the ability of their children to learn basic math and reading. Indigenous Kemetic immigrants born on the continent of Al-Kebulan-Africa became employed in the Social Services agencies.

This change has created a double challenge because Kemetic Americans have a professional interest in reaching our career objectives. We are also interested in using our capacity to affect positive change in our communities. I had the inner motivation to seek evidence-based answers to and solutions around the level of

HIV/AIDS infection. Sons and daughters of Kemet, the largest growing ethnic group, were being infected. Their families had a double challenge because they were disproportionately affected by the disease. I was especially interested in understanding heterosexual infection among women of color whom their male partners infected.

We have more of a commitment than those of other ethnicities who may support the belief that we are inherently inferior. They are unaware of our struggles and achievements despite and against all social and political odds. If they are from India or the Middle East, they are culturally infused with a social caste system, influencing their interactions across ethnic groups. They identify with Europeans and consider themselves Aryan despite their dark skin.

Many individuals from India have entered the medical field as doctors, nurses, and physician assistants. I have personally heard of an incident from my family member. Doctors and medical personnel were speaking in the language, "Farsi," over the head of my stepson, who had been diagnosed with cancer. In other incidents, they refused even to touch Kemetic descendants while providing care.

This is a caste-delineated reality in their culture. I speak these truths and open a new dialogue based on fact with limited emotion. Let us examine this issue more closely. Political decisions are currently being made around the question of immigration. This is not just a Mexican border issue. It continues to impact our culture and harmonious survival! There was a large influx of immigrants into Queens County between 2015 and 2019.

See Table 5: Queens County Immigrant Population Expansion 2015-2019.

**Table 5: Queens County Immigrant Population Expansion 2015-2019**

| COUNTRY OF ORIGIN | TOTALS 2015/2019 |
|---|---|
| China (includes Taiwan, Hong Kong) | 170,000 |
| Bangladesh | 54,800 |
| Jamaica, West Indies | 49,000 |
| India | 47,200 |
| Central America (not including Mexico) | 44,200 |
| Philippines | 34,500 |
| Trinidad & Tobago | 26,000 |
| Pakistan | 13,800 |
| Ukraine | 5,300 |
| TOTAL | 444,800 |

https://www.migrationpolicy.org/search?search_api_views_fulltext=Population+by+state+and+county&field_publication_type=All&created%5Bdate%5D=09%2F01%2F2001&created_1%5Bdate%5D=

I recently returned to Jamaica, NY after an eight-year absence to see the formerly white neighborhood of Jamaica Hills and its adjacent commercial strip along Hillside Avenue completely converted to an ethnic Middle Eastern community, mainly from Bangladesh and India. They had expanded the size of their homes, built mosques and schools, and acquired ownership of many large apartment buildings with corresponding storefronts. They hired their sons and daughters to work in these businesses. So, Kemetic Americans do not get jobs in these businesses that draw every dollar they can get from our pockets.

Many of them immigrated with money. However, I believe they also pooled their professional resources from employment and purchased predominantly Jewish establishments in three years–according to a community contact. It goes even deeper than that! Many can receive United States Federal business development loans and grants to open shops in our neighborhoods.

However, the most significant break is the huge immigrant business seven-year tax abatements, effective until they become naturalized. The seven-year limit gets extended when they transfer ownership to a new immigrant relative, who continues to receive the seven-year tax abatement for the same business.

Some immigrants have relatives who own warehouses in Bangladesh, China, and Thailand from whom they can receive shipments at wholesale prices. Kemetics purchase these goods at 99 Cent Stores, Dollar Stores, and Hair Supply stores opening up on every corner in our neighborhoods. They are now beginning to open stores along the Jamaica Avenue commercial strip. I am not mad at them, either! We are the ones who have been sleeping like Rip Van Winkle!

See Table 6: Total Population Queens County 2,270,976[9]

**Table 6: Total Population Queens County, 2,270,976**

| RACE & HISPANIC ORIGIN | POPULATION |
| --- | --- |
| One Race Total Population | 2,136,976 |
| White | 815,280 |
| Black or African American | 411,046 |
| American Indian & Alaska Native | 11,354 |
| Asian | 588,182 |
| Native Hawaiian et al. Pacific Isle | 2,270 |
| Some Other Race | 311,123 |
| Two or More Races | 133,987 |
| Hispanic or Latino origin (all races) | 631,335 |

Take a look at the two tables. Table 5 shows the huge influx of immigrants who came into Queens pre-Covid between 2015 and 2019, totaling 441,000 people. Now, look at Table 6: Black or African Americans total 411,046 people. The total number of Immigrants is 444,800.

---

9      U.S. Census Bureau 2020 demographics for Queens, NY: https://data.census.gov/table?q=2020+Queens+County,+NY+Popu+lation+by+Race

The reason I present this comparison is a political issue. Kemetic Mayor Eric Adams failed to implement a local law that would allow more than 800,000 non-citizens to vote in local New York City elections. "Four Black registered voters in the city represented by the Public Interest Legal Foundation (PILF) alleged that the law was motivated by racially discriminatory intent that violates the Voting Rights Act."

The article, "Conservatives' Federal Case Challenges Immigrant Voting–Using Ex-Council Member's Own Words," was written by Yoav Gonen, a writer for an online publication, dated August 30, 2022. This decision caused an Indiana-based law firm to file a lawsuit in Federal Court to prevent the law from going into effect. The argument of racial bias is very relevant because voters can influence where local resources would be prioritized for special programs and economic development initiatives. Hispanic and Asian groups would likely make decisions that were not in the interest of Kemetic (African) Americans.

Southeast Queens is surrounded by a circle of prosperity where immigrant ethnic groups reside. Twenty years of properties/business development lying fallow have made this area vulnerable to banks and finance companies in the process of gentrifying our neighborhood to our detriment.

Let us return to the case of Jamaica, southeast Queens. Twenty years of commercial properties lying "fallow" have recently been replaced by banks and other businesses owned mainly by Bengali Indians from India and other Middle-East ethnicities, opening up along the commercial strips of Linden and Merrick Boulevards. Major and minor streets are being re-paved as I write. Home values have increased. But look at this! In the nineteen square miles of Southeast Jamaica, Queens County, New York City, there were 17,537 pre-foreclosures, short sales, sheriff sales, and bank foreclosure homes in March 2023. These homes are owned chiefly by people of Kemetic descent.

Many of the homes in Southeast Jamaica are owned by those who have now become elders in the community and are experiencing the challenges accompanying aging. Their properties deteriorate, and as they seek home improvement loans, the banks undermine them and take advantage of their age by offering and approving thirty-year amortized loans instead. While banks may not discriminate according to age, they take advantage of the older population with this predatory business practice. They use age to their advantage. My mother had an elderly friend who lost her home, and the Chinese family who purchased it locked her out and did not allow her to retrieve her belongings. This is a sad state of affairs for many.

Throughout the years, I witnessed a rotation of ethnic privilege in New York City. The Chinese always operated food shops in inner city communities. Eventually, Koreans operated vegetable shops and fresh fish shops. Latinos were allowed to open "bodegas" as small stores and delicatessens eventually, and Arabs from the Middle East were given the opportunity to open various shops and gasoline-filling stations in our community. The situation has become even more sophisticated with the Bengalis and Indians. They have replaced Kemetic medical doctors in providing care in hospitals and medical facilities.

They have been permitted to open small drug stores providing medical supplies unavailable in the chain "pharmacies." They have a guaranteed customer base who need to purchase supplies or prescriptions that Kemetic community members who are dying off in record numbers need. It is interesting to note that pharmacies acquire a database of properties that may become available because the patient's name, address, date of birth, and disease are linked to each prescription.

The same ethnic members become predatory purchasers of property owned by Kemetic elders who cannot receive home improvement loans, deceived by predatory finance companies using manipulations to acquire properties for higher profit. Reverse mortgage loans are set up by finance companies and supported by Federal Housing and Urban Development agencies.

This has had tragic results for many Kemetic owners, their descendants, and other Americans who become propertyless. Property ownership is linked with land ownership as key objectives here in the United States. Kemetic Americans pay property taxes that become diverted to assist foreigners just arriving in this country.

Palestinians now own the local supermarket. They used to hire mostly other Palestinians as workers – now that has changed. They got the memo and responded! We must look in the mirror and greet "Rip Van Winkle." You can only say this if you have finally awakened. Doing nothing in your community shows that you are still sleeping. Sacrifice your TV time, think, meet with people, and take time to get something done.

A major ethnic controversy occurred between Caribbean descendant parishioners of a church and members of the St. Albans Civic Association and Addisleigh Park Civic Organization. The church wanted to build a housing and community center designed to change the integrity of the neighborhood skyline. It is clear that there is no historical sentiment among recent residents, nor do they have the same priorities for the community. Internal communication and compromise were established in this case, resolving what could have become an inter-ethnic legal battle.

According to Harold Cruse, this is a prime example of the dialectical interplay of material and spiritual culture predicated on the "social reality of group, ethnic, race, and national minority conflicts.

> "…the peculiar history of race and ethnic developments in American history submerges the incipient class conflict under the more pressing and demonstrative impact of group, ethnic, race, national minority conflicts, contentions, and competition for social power and group prestige." Pt. I p. 66

Racial profiling has shifted from gentrified Harlem and Central Brooklyn into Jamaica, Queens. By the time he was twenty-four, our neighbor's son had been stopped three times by police for unknown reasons. In one incident, while he was an employed college student, he was fingerprinted, had his retina scanned, and was detained overnight for "unknown" reasons! His godfather, grandmother, and mother – all formidable people – stood with him as the Judge asked, "Why are you here?" There is a need to replace at least five of the zip codes of youth targeted for processing into Riker's Island and the State prison system, as Jamaica has been identified as a new area for housing and business development.

Health disparities continue to tremendously impact Kemetic families living in the United States throughout the years. A flier distributed by the U.S. Department of Health and Human Services defines health disparities as the "differences in health outcomes closely linked with social, economic, and environmental disadvantages that are often driven by the social conditions in which individuals live, learn, work, and play." We need to know what we are up against in order for us to plan activities so that we can Save-Our-Selves.

There was a time when we were in the care of Kemetic doctors, and we got our prescriptions filled by Kemetic pharmacists. We had so much trust in them that we would set our appointments months ahead to be seen by them for medical care. There were many other trustworthy doctors of various ethnicities serving patients in our inner cities who cared for and treated us with integrity. Our health would stabilize or improve under their care. Our doctors had practices with all kinds of expensive medical equipment. All of a sudden, our trusted care people were gone! One would look around a healthcare facility and not see a single Kemetic (Black) doctor.

It has recently come to my attention that nationwide, more than 1,450 medical personnel of all ethnicities– doctors, dentists, or pharmacists mostly serving inner-city communities, have been prosecuted or convicted for "misappropriating" pain medications.

They were charged with the Controlled Substance Act, became targets of the "War on Drugs," and were forced to be victims of civil forfeiture laws.

"**Civil forfeiture** allows the government (typically the police) to seize—and then keep or sell—any property allegedly involved in a crime or illegal activity. Owners need not ever be arrested or convicted of a crime for their cash, cars, real estate, or businesses to be taken away permanently by the government." How, then, can they afford the legal expenses to dispute the charges?[10]"

These developments were brought to my attention in a community discussion, "The Attack on Black Medical Professionals – Is it Real, How Bad is it, & How Does it Affect You and Your Children?" with experts in the field of medicine. This is all tied to covert and overt aggressions denying Kemetic opportunities to maintain our selves, families and communities to reinforce our abilities to thrive. The best and the brightest, well-respected, exceptional medical providers as leaders in the community have had their reputations and property destroyed. This is all connected to regulatory racism and professional lynching.

Medical doctors are licensed by the State where they practice. Similar incidents are occurring nationwide. Most of those indicted were seeing minority patients, and the targeting appears to be based on zip codes. The Drug Enforcement Administration (DEA) conducts its own Court. The State of Texas is a case in point. An unbiased investigation will reveal a concerted effort to remove all Kemetic doctors, dentists, and pharmacists in Texas.

I mention these incidents because no one appears to be concerned about the pain that Kemetic (Black) people experience. It has been well-documented that there are racial disparities in pain management. If our licensed and pain management certified healthcare providers are being prosecuted for pain management care, this negatively impacts our well-being. Patients may be able to

---

10      Cornell Law School. (n.d.). Civil Forfeiture. https://www.law.cornell.edu/wex/civil_forfeiture

share similar experiences amongst themselves. These incidents do not happen in isolation. We must become aware of social patterns that repeat themselves with a different face, destabilizing Kemetic communities and our ability to Save-Our-Selves.

> For more information, search and visit: Black Americans are Systematically Under-Treated for Pain. Why? batten.virginia.edu/about/news/black-americans-are-systematically-under-treated-pain-why
>
> Or, "Taking Black Pain Seriously" www.nejm.org/doi/full/10.1056/NEJMpv2024759

Several government agencies, acting in collusion with one another, operate in a web of mutual channels to snare, and strategize sealing arrests, which ensures eventual prosecution and indictments against professional Medical Doctors, Dentists, and Pharmacists. Similar to the false and overworked narrative on crime, the War on Drugs laws are perpetrated, but not against street-level pushers or the huge drug cartels.

An authentic, effective, and efficient Drug Enforcement Agency would target the huge drug cartels that manufacture illicit drugs and export them into port cities for distribution by low-level dealers into communities, mainly via the Interstate Highway system, harming all U.S. Citizens. Medical professionals who serve our communities have a high ethical standing and care about the health and well-being of their patients. Some are licensed to provide chronic pain treatment. Over the years, they accumulate expensive medical equipment, assets of cars, offices, and real estate property, and after all is conveniently confiscated, medical professionals have no resources to afford the necessary legal fees to plead their cases.

It has become more convenient and safe to storm a Kemetic-owned office or drug store in the community than to stalk the jungle or comb the waterfront to stop the source of trafficking. Locally, immigrants can open small drug stores even less than a block from the large chain stores. Is the strategy for them to replace our Kemetic-owned pharmacies?

"Under the authority of the Controlled Substance Act, the Drug Enforcement Agency and its Diversion Control Program have a Tactical Diversion Squad. Their Investigators have the authority to conduct investigations of doctor's offices. This criminal enforcement wing combines resources and expertise to identify, target, investigate, disrupt and dismantle individuals or organizations involved in diversion schemes. They participate in purchasing evidence, payment for information, surveillance, undercover operations, and executing search warrants when working cases against "overprescribing doctors." [CITATION Mil18\l 1033]

The medical professional presenters at the New York City community forum shared that there are 400 Kemetic doctors indicted and jailed for medical fraud. Most of the charges were related to the FDA-approved, legally prescribed narcotic analgesics (opioids) as pain medications. Pain patients are known to take prescription drugs and resort to street drugs if their prescription drugs are reduced or unavailable.

"CDC found the highest rates of fentanyl overdose were in the northeast, with much of New England- including Maine, Massachusetts, New Hampshire, and Rhode Island– reporting 60 to 90 percent of opioid overdose deaths involving fentanyl. Among these opioid deaths, non-Hispanic white men aged 25 to 40 had the greatest representation. Cutting purer, weaker drugs with synthetic opioids has resulted in a sharp rise in fatal overdoses as street dealers with little grasp on appropriate dosing sell mislabeled opioids to unsuspecting users" (2017, O'Donnell et al.).

At this writing, legal concerns around Medical Doctors, Dentists and Pharmacists who provide pain treatment have reached the Supreme Court. According to Docket #22-6000, Norman J. Clement vs. the Drug Enforcement Administration, the case challenges the authority of the DEA to issue guidelines that constitute advice relating to the general practice of medicine or to create new laws and regulations about treating pain.

Now take a look at the schools. Many students are not studying, doing homework, or reading books. There are fewer and fewer young Kemetic descendants graduating high school. What's up with that? They have their heads in digital "idiot boxes," blipping and blinking their way through life. Put them on quiet time. As mentioned earlier, these electronic devices are dangerous, especially for the brains of developing babies, children, and teens. Everybody stop! Have a local collective plan!

Research on children and the amount of behavioral and psychological effects of the screen time they experience has become a growing concern for many parents. On December 13, 2022, Elizabeth Chuck, a reporter for NBC News, presented recent research results documenting higher rates due to long-term risks of "obsessive-compulsive disorder among preteens." Another study investigated the extent to which children can calm themselves when they become upset over life's challenges[11].

Get over whatever issues you may have with friends and family and see how to combine resources to ensure your personal and group survival. Now is the time to begin! Go to the home of your elder and ask for their forgiveness. Ask if you can help them in exchange for being their apprentice.

Be able to give help and accept help. Cultivate forgiveness and healing so that we can move forward together. From this moment on, expand human relations between all people, all parents, all partners, friends, adults, and children.

Say the Ho' Oponopono chant taught by Ihaleakala Hew Len, Ph.D., that comes from indigenous Hawaiian culture. You can say or chant these phrases in any order:
- "I Love You"
- "I'm Sorry"

---

11        Chuck, E. (2023, August 18). Research finds more negative effects of screen time on kids, including higher risk of OCD. NBC News. https://www.nbcnews.com/health/kids-health/negative-effects-screen-time-kids-rcna61316

- "Please Forgive Me"
- "I Thank You"

Don't apologize to them LIKE you really mean it. Absolutely, REALLY MEAN IT!

Ask what you can do to help them. Ask if their taxes are up to date. If they are under eighty-five years old in New York State or under seventy-five in other states, ask if they have enough life insurance to cover the debt on the house if they own a home. If they don't have the coverage, encourage them to find someone they can trust and acquire the necessary life insurance on the property to discourage the automatic acquisition by banks and finance companies.

If they have a pension, ask whether they have assigned a transfer-of-ownership of the pension to someone for the time when they are no longer with us. Some cultures take out an insurance policy on the oldest living member in their family below seventy-five. Take advantage of this opportunity, allowable by law in the United States.

Families need to avoid the expenses of Probate Court between the State and Family members by putting all of their elder's assets in a trust. Settle issues out of Court. These practices help assure the economic longevity of surviving family members and protect the assets our elders have built up over the years. Ownership of real estate property is essential throughout the United States. It is one of the main objectives for family prosperity.

A key solution for Kemetic descendants living in America is to expand the institution of family. Cultivate relationships between the man, woman, and child; father, mother, and children; "Emperor and Empress; Prince and Princess; Fathers and Mothers" to strengthen our covenant to Save-Our-Selves.

# SOURCES

*"Black and White: Outlines of the next stage"*
Cruse, H. (1971). In Black World, January, 1971, p. 66

*Zerolimits: The Secret Hawaiian System for Wealth, Health, Peace & More.*
Vitale, Joe & Hew Len, Ihaleakala, Ph.D. (2007). John Wiley & Sons, Inc.: Hoboken, New Jersey.

*Morbidity and Mortality Weekly Report*
O'Donnell, J.K., Ph.D. et al., Deaths Involving Fentanyl, Fentanyl Analogs, and U-47700 – 10 States July to December 2016, (2017)

U.S. Census Bureau, June 30, 2022. Accessed at http:// wonder.cdc.gov on 12-5-2022

Want more information?  Go to my website:
Jamaica "Downtown" Revitalization Initiative
https://www.pinealpinecones.com/article/jamaica-downtown-revitalization-initiative

# CHAPTER SIX

## *Life in Our Father's House*

*Light, Peace, Progress, and Power to the 29,869,475* (**workforce population**) *non-institutionalized, Kemetic American Men between the ages of 15 and 65 who live, study and work to support their families every day – just like Our Dad!*
CDC Wonder, U.S. Census (6-30-2022)

- Our Dad was an artist, musician, and educator and the sole provider of a wife and five children until our youngest sister was fourteen years old.
- Life has always had its economic ups and downs.
- We lived in a mutually supportive family environment personified by love and discipline in a mutually supportive social and religious community.
- Our citizenship in the USA is documented as dating back to 1704.
- In addition to the free labor provided by other ancestral lineages, my forefathers have contributed to the development of the United States of America by working and paying our taxes for 307 years.
- My forefathers have contributed to the development of the United States of America by serving in the Armed Forces / Military for 307 years.

Warren L. Harris, Sr. (1917-1988) was an artist, a musician, and a high school educator. As early as I can remember, there was the scent of linseed oil and the sound of primarily classical music at that time, wafting through the house. An artist's smock and a pallet were his everyday attire. Eventually, I had three other siblings besides my older brother. Daddy enjoyed the fact that we could play on the floor and do what children did in his surroundings while he painted. He considered us to be the source of his inspiration. We watched him create sculptures, oils, acrylics, and watercolors. Our family went out on many a picnic, and he would find a scene in nature to paint or sketch while we played, supervised by our mother.

Our family traveled to visit relatives in Philadelphia, Washington, D.C., and Virginia. It seemed like we got dressed up and visited every art museum along the Eastern Seaboard. The experiences became quite boring. It was not until much later in life that I could appreciate the museum trips. Dad would get as close to whatever part of the painting that grabbed his attention and say, "Look, Mattie (my mom), he created the illusion of splashing water like this." Mom would come closer to see, and she would say, "Oh, I see. That's nice."

This was an ever-repeated mantra between them. We learned about all artistic styles, and traditional and modern techniques. We saw "The Thinker" at the Rodin Museum in Philadelphia. That sculpture had a lasting effect on me because I could see that he was really thinking.

I would like to share his story with you because my dad left us a legacy of more than 250 pieces of art, each of which tells its own story. My mother, sisters, brothers, second-generation grandchildren, and I sponsored three major art exhibits after his passing in 1988. We began with the Schenectady Museum and Planetarium in 2004, The African American History Museum in Alexandria, Virginia in 2005 and the main branch of the Brooklyn Public Library at Grand Army Plaza in 2006. Each exhibit came with a busload of family and friends to attend the opening.

His second-generation "great" grandchildren-Dad loved to make punny puns with them-- created a DVD about his history and legacy. My late husband, Ade Olayinka, and I were the executive producers of the project. The 20-minute DVD provided a historical context, and the wrap-around video enhanced the effect of each exhibit.

Warren L. Harris was born in 1917 in Philadelphia, Pennsylvania, to Charles Douglas Morgan and Virdie Estelle Harris. His mother succumbed to Spanish influenza when he was three years old. He was raised in Star Hill, Delaware, by his maternal grandmother, who had ten daughters and one son, and they grew up as siblings. They called him Li'l Warren. From as early as the age of six, he used to make sketches and drawings. He was always kind of quiet. His sisters would ask him to draw a horse and cowboy; he would draw the horse and cowboy. His sisters would give him a bar of ivory or brown soap, and he would whittle a rabbit or another figure out of the soap bar with a pen knife.

As a teenager, Warren was sent to live in Philadelphia with his father, Charles D. Morgan, who played ragtime piano. Granddad later shared with me that he knew Scott Joplin early on and associated with Zoot Sims and Jelly Roll Morton in the 1930s and 40s. I don't want to get too far ahead of the story. Anyway, Dad studied piano under the tutelage of his father as a teenager beginning in 1930. He worked in Granddad's candy store in South Philadelphia and continued to sketch and paint portraits and different scenes of interest in his surroundings.

One memorable day in 1934, while working at the counter, a special guest, Mr. George Schuyler, an influential Kemetic Conservative Editor for the *Pittsburgh Courier,* was one of the customers. Mr. Schuyler was so impressed that he wrote an editorial in his *Views and Reviews* column:

> "Wherever you go in this country you will run across some unknown-colored person who stands out from the ruck of human beings.
>
> The other day while in Philadelphia, I chanced into a little candy store at 1707 Lombard Street. To my surprise, I noticed that half of one wall of the place was covered with unusually fine watercolors and crayons.
>
> Among them were several portraits revealing such admirable sense of character, delineation, coloring, and

knowledge of anatomy as to be worthy of mention in any ordinary art exhibit. Many of them indeed, far outclassed a number of pieces I have seen displayed either at the Harmon Foundation's exhibits of works by Negro artists or at some of the more significant and important exhibits in large galleries in New York.

The clerk, a slender dark youth with intelligent, sensitive features, admitted modestly that he was the painter; that he was but 16 years old, and has been attending art classes for some time. His name is Warren Harris. Here is talent that Philadelphia should aid, and encourage, and probably will."

The same year, Warren joined Philadelphia's Graphic Sketch Club. Warren soon returned to Brownsville, Brooklyn, to help support his grandmother and her family during the height of the Depression. Warren moved his date of birth back one year to 1916 so that he could qualify for a Works Progress Administration job. He was hired as a WPA Draughtsman and had the fortunate opportunity to be exposed to the WPA Harlem Renaissance Artists such as Romare Bearden, Charles White, Hale Woodruff, Palmer Hayden, Elizabeth Catlett, Richmond Barthe', Aaron Douglas, William Artis, and the Delaney Brothers – Beauford and Joseph. He responsibly took care of his grandmother and sisters during those hard times.

Warren Harris was so well-trained as a draftsman that he was appointed Junior Engineering Draftsman at the Naval Torpedo Station during World War II and was stationed at Alexandria, Virginia, between 1942 and 1945. The fine precision of his drawings (must have been the melanin) helped the Navy improve the shape and trajectory of the torpedoes, which had a tendency to come up short during naval warfare.

My dad had a major role in solving the problem, so much so that the upper-echelon officers approached his drawing table and looked over his shoulder to ask key questions during their inspection. Warren L. Harris, Sr. is an unsung hero who had a major role in helping the United States and its Allies win the War at sea against Germany. Of course, the two hydrogen bombs took precedence and sealed the victory over Japan.

Dad met our beautiful mother, Mattie, from Dyersburg, Tennessee, while he was stationed in Alexandria, Virginia. This was our sentimental reason for the location of the 2005 exhibit at the Alexandria Black History Museum. They got married and moved to Brooklyn. Dad continued to create paintings and sculptures and became a member of the Committee for the Negro in the Arts based in Harlem.

In 1949, under the directorship of Ms. Mary Beattie Brady, the Harmon Foundation co-sponsored with the James Weldon Johnson Literary Guild, and the New York Public Library, his first major one-man art show at Harlem's Countee Cullen Library. The Harmon Foundation is noted for 46 years (1922-1967) of awarding sons and daughters of Kemet for their distinguished achievement in visual art. Warren Harris continued to proliferate his work and expose his art. Dad received a letter dated April 21, 1950, from the President's Office of Atlanta University in Atlanta, Georgia, which said:

"It gives me great pleasure to notify you that the Jury selected your watercolor 'East River' as the winner of the First Atlanta University Purchase Award of $125.00 at the Ninth Annual Exhibition of Paintings, Sculpture and Prints by Negro Artists. We are glad to have your work represented in our collection of contemporary Negro art…"

Warren L. Harris was eventually compelled to step out of the Artist Environment due to the Communist scare under the influence of Senator McCarthy. He sacrificed refining his craft and receiving accolades to support his family. He later participated in two group exhibits: The Brooklyn Artists March-April 1954 Biennial Exhibition at the Brooklyn Museum and The Village Art Center Eleven Year Retrospective Exhibition of Prizewinners Work at the Whitney Museum that June. By 1967 Warren L. Harris was invited by Dr. Hugh F. Butts, M.D. Chairman of the New York Council of the United Negro College Fund, to join the organizing committee and contribute his art in a fundraising exhibition to be held at the Forum Gallery, "*The Portrayal of Negroes in American Painting.*"

According to Cruse's historical analysis in *The Crisis*, my dad was among the artists who abandoned Harlem to go downtown and integrate with artists in the West Village. My family oral history reveals that an officer in the Committee for the Negro in the Arts was compelled to change his membership name from Warren to William to protect Dad from being permanently blacklisted due to McCarthyism since he had a family to support. As significant events interweave in our histories, our Dad, as an Artist, Educator, Husband, and Father of Five, received his Certificate of Graduation from the Education Department at The University of the State of New York on June 12, 1959.

Warren L. Harris continued to work on major projects with the Board of Education between 1954 and 1983. Mr. Harris mainly taught high school and some junior high, teaching art, mechanical drawing, architecture, and music. His passion for refining his skills in watercolor, collage, oils, marble, wood and clay sculpture remained active.

Warren Harris had an opportunity to take a yearlong sabbatical in 1972 to travel with a group from Pace University, studying the architecture of ancient Greece and Rome. Dad was able to visit the Louvre Museum in Paris, and with paint and pallet in hand, he returned with "studies" that soon became an inspiration to refine the innovative masterpieces created with his all-paper collage technique.

His works were published in (1976) *The International Library of Afro-American Life and History* by the Publishers Agency under the auspices of the Association for the study of Afro-American Life and History. In 1981, another reference, *250 Years of Afro-American Art: An Annotated Bibliography* edited by Lynn Moody Igoe, was published by R.R. Bowker Company.

**And then there was the music...**

When my siblings and I were six years old, we were required to study the piano. Some of us lasted longer than others. I started again in the seventh grade after seeing and hearing my friend JoAnne play "Minuet in G" by Paderewski. I just had to learn that beautiful piece. There was always live music in our house.

Our elementary school, P.S. 36 Queens, introduced string violin classes for third and fourth graders. My younger brother Geoffrey was in the fourth grade, and he learned string bass by playing the bottom with a bow while another boy stood on a chair and held the frets at the top. Then, they would switch positions. Eleanor started on the violin when she reached third grade. My older brother Warren, Jr. acquired a trombone and baby sis, Karen, learned clarinet.

I did not receive my second instrument until I registered for the Beginning Band at Forest Hills High. I asked for the flute. Mr. Pollack, the band teacher, asked me to sing some notes and told me he had enough flute players in the band and that I would play the bassoon. All summer long, I thought it was the size of an oboe. Wasn't I surprised to have an instrument that came up to my chin when standing up!

Well, we all played music together, mostly on a Sunday afternoon. I must admit that we bored our visiting relatives and friends until we gradually improved. We played jazz, rock, gospels, spirituals, and some classical pieces together. When our friends came over, Dad played the piano while we sang.

Dad was an excellent chef. He often would come home from work, put on his apron and make biscuits. My junior high buddies would ride their bikes over from Hollis, smell the biscuits in the oven, and ask Mr. Harris for hot biscuits with butter. I had to wait until dinner was ready to get a biscuit. My brother had to write a simile for homework when he was in the fourth grade. He wrote the sentence, "As good as Dad's spaghetti."

Dad made the best peach cobbler and homemade pie crust in the world. He learned the recipe from our great-aunt, Anoh, while sitting with her and watching her every move as she prepared each step, measuring the ingredients with her hands. He set a peach cobbler standard that is still hard to replicate. Great-aunt Anoh taught Dad how to make yeast rolls, which he rocked on many a holiday. It was "all she wrote" when Daddy mastered dessert and dinner crepes from a cookbook. These were just a few of his specialties in the kitchen.

Dad started making biscuits because he "felt sorry for our mother who had all five of us in the house all day long." For the most part, mom was a homemaker until our youngest sister became 14 years old. Even then, we were a unique family. Many of our friends thought we took so long to eat dinner because we didn't want them to know there wasn't enough food in the house.

Truth be told, we had a lot to share about our day around the table. Most families in Addisleigh Park had both parents working, or were on the verge of or already divorced. Daddy could "burn" in the kitchen, and it had nothing to do with preconceived notions of his "manhood."

Many of our friends would come to the house to visit our father instead of us. They would even tell us this. Dad would talk to them about the beauty of full lips and broad noses and the musical inflections in the Southern accent. He would talk about the pride we should have in our "African" heritage. The boys would come with different questions about art and music. Our friends recognized his empathy and caring and gravitated to his counsel. My good high school buddy, Gloria, always told me it was the biscuits and the music. She would ask him to play "Malagueña," and we would listen to an awesome personal concert just for the two of us while the biscuits were baking.

Mom was a "Scout Mom." There was a time when each of us were members of the Brownie, Cub, Girl, Senior Girl, and Explorer Scouts. Imagine trying to keep up with all those activities and the badges we earned! Mom would have my sisters and me read poetry while she braided our hair. We learned about all the classical European poetical works too numerous to name at this time. I eventually became exposed to the works of Kemetic-descended Harlem Renaissance poets while attending college.

Mom was also spontaneous with her teaching. One day, our friend Claudette came across the street looking for us to play with, and we were not home. My mother said, "Come in. I want to show you something." Claudette learned how to upholster a chair. Twenty years later, after moving out of town, she came over to thank my Mom for teaching her how to do something as a skill she continued to apply all her life.

Mom always surprised us with new draperies, curtains, or furniture covers when we came home from school. It's no wonder that every Christmas, Dad would purchase two outfits for her from Bloomingdales to wear whenever they attended cocktails, receptions or dinners that coming year. "Oh, Warren, this is too much money," she would say. Smoking cherry tobacco in one of his many pipes, he said, "I want it for you. You deserve nice things."

## The Harris Tribal Heritage

We have records that my family dates back to 1704 through our paternal Forefather, William Harris. Two of my cousins, Martha Alexander Paskins and Angel McKnight, engaged in a family history and ancestor search, which resulted in the publication of a book, *Progeny Meet Destiny: The Kindred Connection*. It is written as the *Harris Family Genealogy, Historical and Commemorative Book*. Two incidents involving my forefathers took place during the time of the Civil War between 1861 and 1865.

Our forefather, Enoch D. Harris, was born a free descendant of Kemet in 1836, and according to the U.S. Civil War Draft Registration Records 1863-1865, he served in the Delaware 23rd Colored Infantry of the Union Army. His wife was LuJane Summers, a slave. His Father-in-law was Vincent Summers, a free man who had land near Willow Grove in Kent County, Delaware. He had an AME Church/meeting house built on his property. Vincent Summers was known for urging our people to stand up for their rights, as even then, he stood up against racial oppression.

On August 28, 1862, a party of white citizens who lived in the neighborhood burned the AME Church meeting house to the ground. The lynch mob visited Vincent Summers's home to hang him and found that he was not home. Vincent was relatively well off and was eventually forced to leave his land and property, which caused him economic hardship, resulting in the confiscation of his property due to delinquent taxes. This incident very likely inspired Great-Grandfather Enoch Harris to join the Union Army to fight against slavery. Vincent Summers eventually moved to Star Hill, just outside of Dover. Star Hill was "owned" by Quakers, who gave the land to free Kemetics as a safe place for their families to live.

Millions of descendants of Kemet residing in the United States have similar histories. Eight generations of our families fought hard and well and adapted to life here in the U.S., despite entrenched economic hardship and social degradation, paid their taxes. We are American Citizens. We care about this country. We are not your enemies. We are seeking opportunities for ourselves and our families. The crimes they attribute to Kemetic Americans and the fear they engender are over-exaggerated in the media.

# SOURCES

U.S. Census Bureau, June 30, 2022. Accessed at http:// wonder.cdc.gov on 12-5-2022

*The International Library of Afro- American Life and History*
AALH. (1976) by the Publishers Agency under the auspices of the Association for the study of Afro- American Life and History.

*250 Years of Afro- American Art: An Annotated Bibliography*
Igoe, Lynn M., Ed. (1981). R.R. Bowker Company: New York.

*Progeny Meet Destiny: The Kindred Connection*
Paskins, Martha A. (2016). Publisher: DiggyPOD.com, Tecumseh, MI. pgs. 21-24

McKnight, Angel. Ancestor Search Consultant

# CHAPTER SEVEN

## *The Family – Targeted Impacts on the Survival of Our Future Generations*

- Chemtrails affect Family Health and Well-Being

In spite of Civil Rights and Black Power policy shifts, Black Lives Still Matter. Everyone wants to migrate to the United States; many experience challenges when they enter, and eventually, their families prosper. The best and the brightest leave their homelands, professional and intellectual deserts bereft of their own proactive citizens committed to improving the lives of their own countrymen and women.

### Chemtrail Radiations

Our battle is mental. Our families are impacted. We are compelled to use our collective minds and bodies to Save-Our-Selves. Many of us are becoming aware that the radiation from the chemtrail streaks in the sky is designed to cause us to be angry and generate angst, making us fight one another, and we don't even know why. So, we stop fighting and name-calling.

Chemtrails create clouds that block sunlight from all humans, plants, and animals. The clouds of chemicals are sprayed like exhaust from airplanes and spread across the sky above. Sunlight heats the artificial clouds, allowing radiations of toxic chemical, microscopic droplets to fall to the Earth. The chemicals that are most mentioned include Cadmium, Strontium, and Barium. I mention this reality and briefly illustrate how they each impact our ability to "Save-Our-Selves." I suggest that you simply search online: "What do chemtrails contain? What dangers are chemicals to humans? What is toxicity? Find out about aluminum. Interestingly, some of these biological effects are very similar to Covid-19 symptoms – "I'm Just Saying" (I-J-S).

**Cadmium:** "Acute inhalation or high levels of exposure of cadmium over a short period of time can result in flu-like symptoms (chills, fever, and muscle pain) and can damage the lungs. Chronic or low-level exposure over an extended period of time can result in kidney, bone, and lung disease.[12]"

**Strontium:** "Exposure to stable or radioactive strontium occurs from ingesting contaminated food, drinking water or breathing contaminated air. In children, high levels of stable strontium can impair bone growth. High levels of radioactive strontium can cause anemia or cancer." ToxFAQs™: Strontium –ATSDR

**Barium:** "A small amount of water-soluble barium may cause a person to experience breathing difficulties, increased blood pressure, heart rhythm changes, stomach irritation, muscle weakness, changes in nerve reflexes, swelling of brains and liver, kidney and heart damage."

www.atsdr.cdc.gov www.lenntech.com

Chemtrails have also been found to contain toxic levels of Mercury. The first five out of 42 emotional effects of mercury include:

- anxiety
- depression
- suicidal thoughts
- panic attacks
- anger, short temper, sudden outbursts of emotion, rage.

It's important to "follow the Science" to deny the attempts by others to label these realities as "conspiracy theories."

www.ncbi.nlm.nih.gov › pmc › articles › PMC4555286

Dr. J. Marvin Herndon, Ph.D., author of (2015) "Evidence of Coal-Fly-Ash Toxic Chemical Geoengineering in the Troposphere: Consequences for Public Health," [ CITATION Herne \l 1033] introduces his findings in the Abstract:

---

12    What Health Effects Are Associated With Acute High-Dose Cadmium Exposure? The CDC's Agency for Toxic Substances and Disease Registry: https://www.atsdr.cdc.gov/csem/cadmium/Acute-Effects.html

"The widespread, intentional and increasingly frequent chemical emplacement in the troposphere has gone unidentified and unremarked in the scientific literature for years. The author presents evidence that toxic coal combustion fly ash is the most likely aerosolized particulate sprayed by tanker jets for geoengineering, weather-modification and climate-modification purposes and describes some of the multifold consequences on public health."

The Covid-19 Global Pandemic and mandated social quarantine negatively impacted the institution of family in the United States. The population of unemployed individuals has totaled 40,000,000. I have compiled a number of online resources documenting the impact of Covid-19 on Kemetic Americans and other communities of color. Remember that Kemetic Americans make up only 13.4% (89,922,562) of the total population (663,394,936) in the United States. (see p. 150) This shows that our overall population has remained stagnant over the years, while others have experienced positive growth and development.

This total includes all races labeled as Black/African American in the U.S. census. Our actual population is steadily decreasing. Let us concentrate on strategies to Save-Our-Selves. The following information presents a snapshot of the crisis impacting Kemetic individuals, families, and communities.

Corona-19 Virus USA Jan. 21, 2020, through September 21, 2022 Source: Johns Hopkins University-https://corona virus.jhu.edu/

**Table 7: COVID-19 Virus USA January, 2020 through September, 2022**

| Total Cases | 96,551,323 |
| --- | --- |
| Total Deaths | 1,061,478 |
| Total Black  **13.75%** | 146,035 |

Sources: Total Cases and Deaths – Johns Hopkins Coronavirus Resource Center Kemetic (Black)Americans APM Research Labs
https://www.apmresearchlab.org/covid/deaths-by-race

The key to Table 7 is that according to the current data collection system, Kemetic Americans normally make up approximately 13% of the total population who died directly from COVID-19 infection. This data 146,035 shows that approximately 13.75% of all deaths from the COVID-19 virus were Kemetic Americans. Other causes, like heart disease, diabetes, and cancer are no longer in the equation. There is finally a distinction between dying directly from COVID-19 and people with other diseases who became vulnerable and died with COVID-19 infection.

I would like to believe that these are accurate numbers. The inflated numbers and repeated images in the media caused people to panic throughout the pandemic. Including Hispanic, Indigenous, and Asian populations would also increase the Covid death percentages. Issues regarding structural racism became apparent as they came to the forefront when attempting to explain health disparities.

Structural racism has become a "tag word" in the social sciences to toss responsibility for quality care or service provision from one agency to another. In this case, the term is used by the New York City Department of Health and Mental Hygiene to explain the "Health Inequities" in their Covid Data.

> "Structural racism --- centuries of racist policies and discriminatory practices across institutions, including government agencies, and society - - prevents communities of color from accessing vital resources (such as health care, housing, and food) and opportunities (such as employment and education), and negatively affects overall health and well-being. The disproportionate impact of COVID-19 on New Yorkers of color highlights how these inequities negatively influence health outcomes."

They do present the Department of Health and Mental Hygiene's COVID-19 Equity Action Plan. They will: "Engage with healthcare providers; Engage with community partners; and communicate with the community." There is no mention about the other public health concerns or to collaborate with other agencies within or external to the department in the interest of the community at large.

I invite Community members as Solutions Specialists to explore the different hyperlinks to help families and friends resolve key challenges that we confront every day. The Joint Center compiled the following sources to address impacts on Communities of Color. Although some links may not be live, the parent organizations have updated information relevant to major topics of interest.

**The Kaiser Family Foundation** just reviewed various studies on race and COVID-19 and found that "Black mortality rates were over twice as high as white mortality rates and age-adjusted hospitalization rates for African Americans were almost five times higher than whites. The Kaiser study also cited a Harvard report that shows that between February 1 and May 20, **African Americans lost more years of potential life than whites (45,777 years vs. 33,446 years)**, even though the overall African American population in the U.S. is much smaller."

**The Center for American Progress** evaluated how the wealth gap could cause Black children to fall behind in school access, stating that "due to systemic racism in the housing industry, predominantly Black neighborhoods tend to have lower property values. This, in turn, means the schools in these same neighborhoods have fewer financial resources—and these financial pressures have only increased and made racial inequities worse since the pandemic.[13]"

Other social impacts include job loss and concurrent loss of mortgage and rental housing. Many cities have reported pushback moratoriums on foreclosures and evictions through January 15, 2022[14].

---

13      Francis, D., & Weller, C. E. (2020, August 12). The Black-White Wealth Gap Will Widen Educational Disparities During the Coronavirus Pandemic. American Progress. https://www.americanprogress.org/article/black-white-wealth-gap-will-widen-educational-disparities-coronavirus-pandemic/
14      Joint Center for Political and Economic Studies. (2020, August 18). August 18 COVID-19 Policy & Black Communities Roundup. https://jointcenter.org/august-18-covid-19-policy-black-communities-roundup/

Just like the virus's outsize impact on the health of communities of color, the unemployment crisis is in several ways worse among Black Americans, who are disproportionately more likely to be unemployed but are also least likely to receive jobless benefits.

On September 30, 2020, The National Low-Income Housing Coalition convened a webinar, "Preventing Evictions for Communities of Color During the Covid- 19 Pandemic." They discussed the following and brainstormed strategies to mitigate the continuing crisis:

"The COVID-19 pandemic and subsequent economic fallout have heightened the threat of eviction for Black and Brown renters, but these risks are not new. The housing crisis and its disproportionate harm to low-income people of color have deepened over the last several decades.

At the same time, Black homeownership declined, and the country's yawning racial gap widened. The ongoing public health and economic crises further exacerbate existing structural inequalities, including housing instability. Black and Native American communities are bearing the brunt of COVID-19 infections and fatalities, and Latinx and Black people are bearing the brunt of historic job losses. Now, Black and Brown renters are at immediate risk of losing their homes.

The National Low-Income Housing Coalition may have resources for families since the federal eviction moratorium has ended. They suggest that immediate action be taken at the state and local levels. Community members are invited to Zoom calls on HoUSed: Universal, Stable, Affordable Housing. A national call occurs on Mondays. Registration is required. Renters will be able to find out the immediate actions they can take to possibly remain housed. More information is available at the website - https://nlihc.org/coronavirus-and-housing-homelessness/national-eviction-moratorium

By August 26, 2021, a delay occurred in the entire distribution of the federal government's $46.55 billion fund through the Federal

Rental Assistance Program. At this time, some renter evictions have been resolved. Funds were intended to help qualified families or "eligible households that cannot pay rent by covering up to 18 months of unpaid rent. To date, however, only $28 billion has been distributed." Renters became increasingly at risk of eviction due to their mounting debt.

The burden of our mortgages, since the foreclosure moratorium was effective until January 15, 2022. This means that evictions and foreclosure proceedings can take place at any time. Many proceedings have already begun. As I mentioned previously, in the 19 square miles of Jamaica in Southeast Queens County, New York City, there were 17,537 pre-foreclosures, short sales, sheriff sales, and bank foreclosure homes in March 2023. The Southeast Jamaica Population total is 339,120 from the 2020 Census. Thirty percent of this population consists of families with children. Education Levels and Job availability negatively affect residents in Jamaica, Queens.

**Table 8: Education Levels: Southeast Jamaica, Queens, NYC - Compared with the National Percentage**

| DEGREE | % | NAT'L % |
| --- | --- | --- |
| Master's Degree or Higher | 7 | 13 |
| Bachelor's Degree or Higher | 15 | 20 |
| Some College or Associates | 27 | 29 |
| High School or Equivalent | 30 | 27 |
| TOTAL | 79 | 89 |
| Less than High School Diploma | 20 | 11 |

Source: https://www.niche.com/places-to-live/n/jamaica-new-york-city-ny/

In most cases, the values of the homes have more than doubled to over $500,000. Multiplying this number by the distressed family households, we can see that the banks will benefit from a $6,270,000,000 (six billion, 270 million dollars) profit on the stress of Kemetic Families in this small area. What about your communities? You can look this up yourselves.

Go to https://www.foreclosurelistings.com/list/zipcode/87540/ and search according to zip code. Then look up the zip code data sources to find out the population in each zip code to get an idea of the number of families in distress in your neighborhood at https://zipdatamaps.com.

This amounts to a serious concern for families in most urban settings. No one is alone in this. Talk with each other everywhere. Housing affordability related to jobs is another major issue of concern.

On August 5, 2022, an article was written by Samantha Subin for CNBC entitled, "Despite a strong jobs report, unemployment inched higher for Black workers in July." She summarized, "The U.S. job market posted strong growth and a decline in unemployment in July, but unemployment ticked higher to [5.6%] among Black workers, further underscoring the ongoing discrepancies in the job market.[15]"

By October 7th, there was no significant change in this daily update at the Bureau of Labor Statistics. This should beg the following questions: Why should there be so much unemployment in 49% of the adult population in Jamaica, Queens, with some college education at the level of an Associates degree or higher? Why should there be so much unemployment? Moreover, why is there no real way to document true employment by race in Jamaica, Queens? This negatively impacts family stability in Southeast Jamaica, Queens.

Statistics are worse in real life. Unemployment data only tracks those receiving unemployment benefits. There is no source for tracking true unemployment. There is no way to track individuals who are not working and no longer receive benefits.

See Table 9: Unemployment Rates USA Civilians by Race, Sex, Age

15  Despite a strong jobs report, unemployment inched higher for Black workers in July, Samantha Subin, August 5, 2022: https://www.cnbc.com/2022/08/05/july-jobs-report-black-workers-see-rise-in-unemployment-.html

**Table 9: Unemployment Rates USA Civilians by Race, Sex, Age, Unemployment Rates (Eff. 11-4-2022)**

| White | Men, 20+ Years | 3.0% |
|---|---|---|
| | Women, 20+ Years | 3.0% |
| | Both Sexes, 16 to 19 Years | 9.6% |
| | | |
| Black | Men, 20+ Years | 5.3% |
| | Women, 20+ Years | 5.8% |
| | Both Sexes, 16 to 19 Years | 16.5% |
| | | |
| Asian | Overall | 2.9% |
| | Men, 20+ Years | |
| | Women, 20+ Years | |
| | Both Sexes, 16 to 19 Years | |

https://www.bls.gov/news.release/empsit.t02.htm

Well, here we go again! I could not locate a similar report at the local county level on employment by race and ethnicity or immigrant status. The Bureau of Labor Statistics (BLS) reports regional data by employers, not population employment. So, I am compelled to infer from Chapter 5, Table 5: Queens County Immigrant Population Expansion 2015-2019, that mostly 320,300 Asian immigrants have benefitted from employment to the detriment of employment for 411,046 Kemetic Americans in Queens County. Although listed as "Asian," this group includes immigrants from China, Taiwan, Hong Kong, Bangladesh, India, Philippines, and Pakistan.

**Table 10: 2.5% Asian Population - Queens County**

| 1 | China (includes Taiwan, Hong Kong) | 170,000 |
|---|---|---|
| 2 | Bangladesh | 54,800 |
| 3 | India | 47,200 |
| 4 | Philippines | 34,500 |
| 5 | Pakistan | 13,800 |
| | TOTAL | 320,300 |

Source: Migration Policy Institute: U.S. Immigrant Population by State and County
https://www.migrationpolicy.org/programs/data-hub/charts/us-immigrant-population-state-and-county

I am presenting the facts as I see them. There is no need for us to react with the same emotion of rudeness and the false sense of superiority many of them present to us when some of us shop on Jamaica Avenue. We do not want to be arrested and detained. "We don't have "no beef" with individual immigrants."

Arrangements are planned and executed by unknown authorities; they are just automatons doing their bidding. It starts with their women– be aggressive– start altercations– get their male associates to intervene–then call the police. Bengalis do this, especially getting a charge if whites are there to witness their unwarranted antagonism right on Jamaica Avenue. There has always been a history of job competition since our arrival in the United States, clearly since Emancipation.

Let us think about this and strategize ways we might collectively Save-Our-Selves. Our folks in other states, counties, cities, and communities face this same travesty of justice. Forewarned is forearmed with mental control and focus on purpose– not to be arrested and detained.

I have given you the hyperlinks. Search these facts for your own communities. I don't have all the answers, and I know it will take more people than myself to figure out some effective solutions for the very survival of our progeny– future generations. When we learn more and share what we learn, collectively, we can begin to make informed decisions since we know what we are up against.

Let us consciously greet one another by projecting the pulsating pineal pinecones in our brains as we plan future projects. Show each other another way. Prepare for a thousand-plus years of Peace on Earth with the activities and strategies we activate to Save-Our-Selves. S-O-S!!!

We have Family histories of ancestors who have experienced,

and we continue to have many heinous attempts to block our progress here in America.

Throughout the years, the media has presented images of negative stereotypes of our people to the World. This is despite the economic and business development. This is despite the education expansion, the brilliant scientific inventions, and the cultural arts: music, visual art, dance, drama, and creative writing. No wonder Toni Morrison could write a novel called The Bluest Eye, which gets placed, among others, on the banned book list to erase these truths and psychological realities from history.

"Critical race theorists hold that racism is inherent in the law and legal institutions of the United States as they function to create and maintain social, economic, and political inequalities between whites and nonwhites, especially African Americans." We, who are descendants of Kemet living in America, experience racism and its effects every day of our lives. This is a reality–not a theory. There is no way to erase the truth.

The focus of this writing remains on 89.9 million African (Kemetic) Americans. Deficits in quality education, housing, and health attest to the negative social impacts of race. Evidence of ethnic manipulation (see Chapter 5) as whole population replacement bears out efforts to "disappear" almost 90 million via economic job deprivation, resulting in mass housing foreclosures and evictions. Our people are either denied loans or pay more than whites for the same products.

The constant subtle barrages of microscopic sprays from chemtrails have negatively affected the mental and physical health of families and communities. Could it be that the mercury in chemtrails may increase the pain intensity in a patient? Could it be that the mercury effects might influence suicide ideation? What if our Medical Doctors (whom we trust) discovered and questioned the feasibility of this potential reality? Our Medical Doctors, Dentists and Pharmacists are experiencing systematic mass lynching, being removed under the guise of socially contrived laws of the "War on Drugs" with regulations carried out by the Drug Enforcement Administration. They denigrate the roles of medical personnel as if they were drug dealers on the street. Our best and brightest then become victims within the Criminal Justice System. The primary premise in this book asks, "What can we do to Save-Our-Selves?

A most recent development takes the attacks on our physicians to a higher urgency: Black physicians at all levels are accused of being "inferior." An attempt is being made to justify systematically eliminating and forcing the removal of health providers of color. For this and other documentation, go to https://www.youarewithinthenorms.com.

I am not a doctor. I am concerned about my own health and well-being and that of my family and community. I continue to investigate the "root causes" of our "social stagnation" compared to other ethnic groups who enter the United States and continue to prosper. One might question how these medical issues relate to pain and pain management. (I.J.S.)

> "All humans are exposed to some level of mercury. Factors that determine the health effects of mercury include the dosage and types of mercury, the route of exposure (inhalation, ingestion, or skin contact), and the age and developmental stage of the host with the unborn child, infant, and young child most susceptible. Elemental [mercuries, sic] are toxic to the central nervous systems and peripheral nervous systems, causing tremors, cognitive effects, neuropathy, and neuromuscular problems… inhalation is the major route of exposure – absorbed into the lungs and diffused into the blood, following inhalation of mercury, the brain and the kidney…with chronic exposure the greater burden of mercury – (concentrates in) the kidney"(2017: Herndon & Whiteside).

The authors conclude, "The deliberate spraying of aerosolized coal fly ash into the atmosphere must be stopped to prevent further mercury contamination of the biosphere. No one has the right, not even the military, to poison the atmosphere and damage the health of humans and other creatures."

## 5G Technology

Implementing 5G technology adds another assault on our well-being: the generation of electromagnetic frequencies (EMFs) that we can say is commonly understood with cell phones. Frequencies were refined and improved over the years from 2G, 3G, and 4G to send and receive sharp communication signals. 5G frequencies are ten times greater than 4G. Many people have learned that holding cell phones to our heads over time can damage brain cells.

Children and babies must be protected from EMFs to prevent effects on their mental and physical development. Chemtrail spray also permeates our bodies. The chemtrail spray that accumulates inside our bodies allows for the more effective targeting and application of electromagnetic fields such as those produced by 5G transmitters. 5G transmitting towers are coming up everywhere in our neighborhoods, streets, and everything labeled "SMART." Just remember, having "Smart" items in our homes is a "Dumb" idea. Not only are the EMF waves permeating our bodies and homes, but they also facilitate surveillance of our every move.

"5G will enable what's known as "The Internet of Things." Not only will internet and cell phone services be faster, but the entire planet can become "smart." We can have smart driverless cars, smart hospitals, smart fridges, smart coffee makers, smart baby diapers and many other smart services that will emerge as a result of 5G technology - especially within the realms of Artificial Intelligence (AI)" (2017: Herndon & Whiteside).

They go on to say, "For the rollout of 5G technology to happen, countless new antennas would need to be put up in our neighborhoods, workplaces, schools and even in our homes. The vast number of antennas required to employ 5G technology will make it impossible to avoid large-scale exposure to the electromagnetic radiation that they emit." Source: "Is 5G Safe?

An Easy-to-Understand Collective Evolution Guide." Search: Collective Evolution.

Here is a bit more on chemtrails directly related to our health. "Exosomes are tiny sacs of fluid that emerge from cells either when we are stressed out or ill. They let the body know when disease is present. Even in the absence of chemtrails, exposure to 5G electromagnetic radiations can induce a state of disease that can alter the state of all body systems, which create or enhance diseases, and generate exosomes."

Peter Kirby, Author and Researcher, explains that the human body is bioelectric and is susceptible to electromagnetic energy. Along with the central nervous system, it is what makes your body similar to a large antenna[16].

His research may give reality to the fact previously discussed in Chapter 4, "Melanin Revisited," that the bioelectricity in Kemetic bodies may be even more enhanced by the presence of melanin. Sons and daughters of Kemet are logically perfect receptors to these electromagnetic frequency (EMF) assaults on our bodies. "So, 5G is enhanced even more and can cause a state of disease in humans, which results in the increased presence of exosomes. According to Dr. Andrew Kaufman, MD, because of the presence of exosomes, positive test results have been misattributed to Coronavirus."

We are witnessing the intersection of race and its social injustices influencing the economic prosperity of medical professionals, with repercussions of potential sophisticated massacres of our people and others, challenged with the lack of quality medical care and the environmental longevity of Planet Earth. Read on my Kemetic people and others; there is more to come.

---

16      Kirby, P. (2016, August 9). Chemtrails and the New Manhattan Project. Kerry Cassidy. https://projectcamelotportal.com/2016/08/09/peter-kirby-chemtrails-the-new-manhattan-project/

# SOURCES

*"Evidence of Coal-Fly-Ash Toxic Geoengineering in the Troposphere: Consequences for Public Health."*
Herndon, J. Marvin (2015). Retracted in: Intl J Environ Res Public Health 2015 September 02; 12(9): 10941 See also: PMC Retraction Policy.

*"Evidence of the biosphere with mercury: Another potential consequence of on-going climate manipulation using aerosolized coal fly ash."*
Herndon, J.M. & Whiteside, M.(2017). Journal of Geography, Environment and Earth Science International. 13(1): 1-11, 2017; Article no. JGEESI.37308 ISSN: 2454-7352

Further Research:
https://www.activistpost.com/2020/06/thecoronavirus-chemtrails-and-5g-connection.html

# CHAPTER EIGHT

*Cultivating Tacticians for Self-Actualization*

### Sankofa in True History of Going Back to Move Forward with a Plan

We have done this before – We can do it again!

- We, who are Brilliant Beyond All Imagination, can use social media to our advantage–digitally doing this bigger and better.
- Remain focused on targeted strategic objectives using mutual cooperation; volunteer your time using this book as a Guide for Solutions Engineers to Know Your Neighborhood and find out specific areas of need.
- Not just nebulous "Housing-where?" "Education- what areas?" "Jobs-what kind?" "Training in what?"
- Collectively putting our Pineal Pinecones together, we can find out for ourselves.
- We will be able to know who can do what, how many, and where, and identify our urgent needs by using real numbers.
- We can build strong foundations for turning this around and make them blossom like Fibonacci's Sequence mentioned in Chapter 4, Melanin Revisited.
- Despite the ever-occurring massacres, lynchings, police murders, assassinations and inculcating laws to incarcerate our medical professionals. Working together --- We Save-Our-Selves.
- Hey, My Kemetic People! **Let's Get This Done!**

## Economic and Political Growth Stifled by Mass Massacres

Beginning with commonly known facts, the Civil War, also known as the War Between the States, occurred between 1861 and 1865. President Abe Lincoln announced freedom for enslaved persons in the rebellious states in the Emancipation Proclamation on January 1, 1863, stating:

> "All persons held as slaves within the rebellious states are and henceforward shall be free." ... The Proclamation announced the acceptance of black men into the Union Army and Navy, enabling the liberated to become liberators. By the end of the war, almost 200,000 black soldiers and sailors had fought for the Union and freedom."

Self-help activities are documented as early as the 1830s. All-Kemetic communities were founded in different parts of the United States and Canada. By the end of the Civil War, there were over 150 communities located in Canada, Ohio, Illinois, Indiana, and Michigan. "Reformers of that period maintained that the most practical way of approaching the problem of Blacks in the U.S. was to provide a positive program of training, education and practical experiences in independent, self-reliant, social, economic, and political life through the creation of these communities." (Berndt, 1977: 17)

These self-help communities were set up like European communes; their purpose was to train the displaced Kemetics (Africans) for complete freedom. They were supported by those who believed that Kemetics could only learn to cope with independence in a separate environment.

During the Civil War across the South, there was a need for the Union Army to deal with Kemetic families who were left behind on property that was abandoned by fleeing whites. The Port-Royal Experiment of the South Carolina Sea Islands was the first Government sponsored settlement that provided shelter, clothes, medicine, and food.

In 1865, Congress passed legislation creating the Freedman's Bureau, which officially began the Reconstruction Period. Laws were enacted to fulfill the need for continuing a federal program to provide relief for the destitute. Federal legislation included the right to vote. The Bureau enforced civil rights and created schools on all levels for almost every need. It attacked the problems of poverty through direct relief and stimulated opposition from businesses and industries demanding a free labor market. "A program of disenfranchisement and pauperization slowly eroded much of the progress freed men had made in education, business and agriculture" (Berndt, 20).

Berndt is putting it mildly. Disenfranchisement and pauperization (causing people to become or remain poor) were enacted by force. From Emancipation in 1863 through the end of the Reconstruction Period in 1877, there were at least 14 recorded incidents of massacres of free and formerly captured unarmed Kemetics, two massacres of Indigenous people and one incident involving Chinese Americans.

These acts of destruction by the design of economic, political, and social destruction of descendants of Kemet living in the United States have continued to this very day.

**Table 11: Records of Race Massacres 1863-1877**

| # | DATE | MASSACRE | LOCATION |
|---|------|----------|----------|
| 1 | 7-13-1863 | New York City Draft Riots and Massacre | White mobs in civil insurrection attacked African American community committing murder, destroying homes, institutions and an orphanage. |
| 2 | 11-29-1864 | Sand Creek, California | Governor orders calvary to attack surrendered Cheyenne and Arapaho Indigenes; White Abolitionist assassinated for reporting this event. |

| # | DATE | MASSACRE | LOCATION |
|---|---|---|---|
| 3 | 4-12-1864 | Fort Pillow, Tennessee | Confederate troops massacred over 500 surrendering majority Kemetic Union soldiers. |
| 4 | 12-9-1864 | Ebenezer Creek, Georgia | Hundreds of enslaved escapees following Gen. Sherman's Army were blocked from crossing the Creek and killed by Confederate soldiers. |
| 5 | 5-13-1866 | Memphis, Tennessee | White civilians and police killed 46 Kemetics and injured many more while burning houses, schools, and churches. |
| 6 | 7-30-1866 | New Orleans, Louisiana | White residents attacked Kemetic marchers on their way to the Constitutional Convention re: Voting. |
| 7 | 9-19-1868 | Camilla (near) Albany, Georgia | Kemetic Americans expelled from elected office marched peacefully; more than a dozen were killed. |
| 8 | 10-25-1868 | St. Bernard Parish, Louisiana | Groups of white men mobilized to suppress the voting rights of more than 50 freedmen dragged from their homes and murdered. |
| 9 | 9-28-1868 | Opelousas, Louisiana | In response to the promotion of voter registration, a vigilante group massacred hundreds. |
| 10 | 10-24-1871 | Los Angeles, Chinatown | A lynch mob of 500 rioted and murdered at least 18 Chinese after a white civilian died in a shootout. |
| 11 | 12-28-1872 | Skeleton Cave, Arizona | The Yapavai people's shelter was attacked by the U.S. Army, trying to force them to reservations. |

| # | DATE | MASSACRE | LOCATION |
|---|------|----------|----------|
| 12 | 4-13-1873 | Colfax Courthouse, Louisiana | The KKK carried this out in response to a Republican victory in the 1872 elections. White League attacks Kemetic politicians and voters. |
| 13 | 11-3-1874 | Barbour County, Alabama | Whites attacked and killed average estimates of at least 200 Kemetic citizens who organized for a Kemetic Sheriff to remain in office. |
| 14 | 12-7-1874 | Vicksburg, Mississippi | 50 Kemetics, three whites, and one white school teacher at a mass meeting of Republicans were indiscriminately killed by white mobs. |
| 15 | 9-4-1875 | Clinton, Mississippi | Charles Caldwell, formerly enslaved and Republican State Senator, organized a political rally attended by more than 1,500 Blacks and about 75 whites, were attacked; 5 Blacks killed and at least 50 more by vigilantes in the days following |
| 16 | 7-8-1876 | Hamburg, South Carolina | During the Race for Governor, whites organized rifle clubs across the state to intimidate white and Black Republicans; the U.S. Army ended the killing spree of over 100 blacks and three whites |

Source: Zinn Education Projects' Massacres in U.S. History
https://www.zinnedproject.org/collection/massacres-us/

The Homestead Act of 1862 gave 160 acres to whites only. Sons and daughters of Kemet never received their "40 Acres and a Mule" promised early in the Reconstruction Period. The land and tools would have made the freedmen economically independent. Some recently freed Kemetic bondsmen and women stayed in the South and were forced into semi-subsistent work as sharecroppers. A sharecropper is a tenant farmer who lives on land owned by someone else and farms the crops for the landowner. The tenant farmer is not paid in cash for his work and only gets a share of the crop for farming the land.

Kemetic families migrated in mass numbers to establish and populate cities in the South, West, and North. In 1879, Henry Adams of Louisiana led 98,000 Kemetics from Mississippi to Kansas. They formed four colonies or townships– Baxter Springs, Morton City, Singleton, and Nicodemus. The townships flourished for a few years, and residents eventually migrated North, seeking better opportunities.

Politicians and skilled workers looking for a better life were the first to migrate to the North. They wanted housing, and education for their children and found jobs in urban factories. Kemetic businesses began to grow in northern and southern cities where banking, insurance, and newspaper companies made the most money. The rise in businesses was due to Kemetic leaders of the Reconstruction Period who strongly encouraged self-help and racial unity.

From as early as the 1880s until 1915, Booker T. Washington was recognized as the acknowledged leader of the descendants of Kemet in the United States. He emphasized individualism within the framework of capitalism. He believed that financial success could be found in agriculture or the trades and encouraged industrial education. Washington also encouraged the establishment of all-black towns. Tuskegee Institute became the first school in the United States to include vocational education in its curriculum.

## Marcus Garvey: Kemetic Free Enterprise

Another early advocate of Kemetic free enterprise was Marcus Garvey, who, like Washington, was a supporter of the capitalist system and viewed capitalism as necessary to the progress of the world. Garvey believed that all Kemetics could only be helped by Kemetics and that only through economic independence from the whites could they attain dignity and real freedom. In 1914, Garvey formed the Universal Negro Improvement Association (UNIA) based in Jamaica, West Indies, for the betterment of Africans at home and abroad.

Together with Booker T. Washington, Garvey believed that blacks must become independent of white capital and operate their own businesses. As fortune would have it, Booker T. Washington died in November 1915, just prior to the arrival of Marcus Garvey into the United States from Jamaica on March 23, 1916. "The proponents of black capital have borrowed ideas from both Washington's pluralism and Garvey's concept of large-scale enterprise" (Berndt, 20).

Soon after he arrived in the U.S., Garvey traveled to 38 states, and everywhere he found the same conditions. By 1919, the UNIA had 30 branches in different cities. He gave speeches and maintained communication using the Negro World newspaper of the UNIA. Marcus Garvey became the most profound leader the Global Kemetic World has ever known prior to, including, and following the phenomenal 11 years he spent in the United States. It has been documented that about 35,000 stockholders paid at least five dollars a share in the Black Star Line Company, totaling $800,000 (more than three-quarters of a million dollars). The New York City Division of the UNIA had an estimated enrollment of 30,000. Garvey boasted of an international UNIA membership of several million.

For the process of behavior change to take place effectively, it is important to include the components of persuasive communication reinforced with active participation. Garvey trained himself in the skills of public speaking. He used first-hand direct contact by traveling to major cities in North, South, Central America, the Caribbean, and Europe. He had direct contact with seamen who traveled elsewhere and made other contacts. He always had the Negro World publication to build the organization.

The UNIA established Liberty Halls in each of the major cities in the United States. They served the needs of the people by providing a place for Sunday worship, Sunday Schools, nightly public meetings and Saturday night entertainment. The Black Cross Nurses organized soup kitchens for the hungry and provided shelters for the homeless. Garvey considered Liberty Halls to be "Shrines of Negro Inspiration."

Using entertainment to proceed with major speeches made the audience receptive to his messages. Garvey exploited the positive image of the "New Negro." He formed the African Orthodox Church and advocated for using Kemetic images for God and Jesus Christ. He spoke about Ethiopia and the greatness that was once Africa's and was destined to be again. He inspired hope in the people and encouraged them to actively participate in the programs of the UNIA. Garvey admonished, "Up, you mighty race. You can accomplish what you will."

There was something for everyone within the sphere of active participation. There were High Officials, a Men's Militia, the Black Cross Nurses for women, and the Juvenile Corps for the Youth. UNIA branches in different major cities had their own marching bands. Each group had its corresponding uniform to increase group identity and local organizational solidarity.

Members of the UNIA were able to anticipate an annual trip to Harlem to attend an International Convention of the Negro Peoples of the World and participate in a major parade. Garvey used cultural activities to increase the people's political awareness and reinforced this with an economic plan.

Garvey formed the Black Star Line Company in 1919 in response to discrimination on ships against both passengers and seamen. Kemetic merchants were dissatisfied with the mistreatment by European ship owners who would leave the African's goods on the shore if they didn't agree to undersell their merchandise. The company purchased three ships by 1920.

In 1923, Marcus Garvey was falsely indicted for using the mail to defraud. He spent three months in The Tombs in New York City and two years and nine months in the Atlanta Penitentiary in Georgia following appeals.

The Negro Factories Corporation was another business enterprise of the Universal Negro Improvement Association (UNIA) established in 1919. It was incorporated in Delaware, capitalized at a million dollars, and offered 200,000 shares of common stock at five dollars a share. The company aimed to build and operate factories to manufacture every marketable commodity in the industrial centers of the United States, West Indies, and Africa. The corporation developed a chain of cooperative groceries, a restaurant, a steam laundry, a tailor and dressmaking shop, a millinery store, and a publishing house.

A fast forward to November 18, 1927, reveals that Garvey received executive clemency from President Calvin Coolidge, who signed a declaration commuting Marcus Garvey's sentence to end immediately. The charges were completely unfounded in an early case of character assassination to negatively impact the success of this master plan. An immediate deportation order accompanied the declaration. Garvey was given a wonderful ovation by the crowds who had rushed to the New Orleans pier to see him off.

In retrospect, Amy Jacques Garvey, author of Garvey and Garveyism, mused that "from its inception, the steamship company was doomed to failure." The ships were overpriced and in poor condition, and the captains were responsible for sabotaging them, forcing the Black Star Line to spend huge fees on their repair. This caused the credibility of Garvey and his followers to decrease. Members of the executive staff committed irresponsible acts to the detriment of the organization due to jealousy and envy.

I had an opportunity to attend a community workshop conducted by a prominent elder and community leader in Brooklyn, Brother Jitu Weusi, a Black Empowerment Advocate. Part of the conversation included an open discussion about individuals who ran for political office and were not elected. He commented emphatically that the real failure was not running at all, not trying to change at whatever level of intended success. Never, ever have in your mind that Marcus Garvey failed. Garvey's followers in the UNIA faithfully supported him throughout his legal ordeals. Many descendants of Garveyites continue to follow critical lessons learned from the philosophies of Marcus Garvey.

Ten more random massacres against freed Kemetic people took place in the northern and southern United States within the 31 years between Reconstruction's end and before the arrival of Marcus Garvey. The issues concerned voting or striking workers, politics and economics.

Garvey's program brought about massive behavior change among Kemetic Americans. Local whites who witnessed these activities reacted with additional paranoia and fear, and acted violently. This interpretive way of seeing history allows us to see parallel events take place and analyze their contemporary activities. Eventually, we go beyond the Tulsa and Rosewood massacres.

The destruction of Rosewood, an economically thriving Kemetic town, occurred in Florida in 1923. The single war internal to the U.S. took place in defense of the enterprises and thriving "Black Wall Street" businesses in Tulsa, Oklahoma, in 1921. The community was decimated by whites who were resentful of Kemetic wealth in the face of white abject poverty in the Midwest. The community of Greenwood in Tulsa, was also known as "Little Africa." Tulsa and Rosewood were among eight massacres during Marcus Garvey's eleven-year tenure in the U.S.

Take a look at Table 12: Records of Race Massacres 1918 – 1923.

*Cultivating Tacticians for Self-Actualization*

**Table 12: Records of Race Massacres 1918 – 1923 (5 Years)**

|   | DATE | MASSACRE | LOCATION |
|---|---|---|---|
| 1 | 1/28/1918 | Porvenir, Texas | 15 Mexican-Americans gathered up door-to-door unarmed, executed by Texas Rangers; 1,920 deeded acres lost and homes destroyed. |
| 2 | **RED SUMMER** 7-19-1919 | Washington, D.C. | White mobs in uniform attack Kemetic American soldiers returning from World War I who organized resistance to the White violence. Thirty-eight were killed from both sides, and 100 injured. Four days later, 2,000 soldiers were called in to suppress the rioting. |
| 3 | 7/27/1919 | Chicago, Illinois | Confrontation began on a segregated Beach; Kemetic teen killed-White man not arrested; escalated almost a week; 23 Bl 16 White killed, thousands black homes looted, many arson. |
| 4 | 9/30/1919 | Elaine, Arkansas | Kemetic farmers met to form a Union to fight for better pay and higher cotton prices. A White mob fired at them; they returned fire in self-defense. Massacre ensued, leaving more than 100 (estimated 800) African Americans dead, 67 indicted for inciting violence, and 12 Black sharecroppers (the Elaine 12) sentenced to death. |

|   | DATE | MASSACRE | LOCATION |
|---|---|---|---|
| 5 | 11/22/1919 | Bogalusa, Louisiana | The Bogalusa Massacre is an example of the violent interracial labor organizing experienced by racist, anti-labor forces in the early 20th century. |
| 6 | 11/2/1920 | Ocoee, Florida | Over 50 Kemetic Americans were killed after going to vote in a small town outside of Orlando. The massacre purged the entire population for over 60 years. |
| 7 | 5/31/1921 | Tulsa, Oklahoma | White Supremacists massacred a thriving Kemetic community. Popularly known as the Black Wall Street. Looted and burned 40 blocks, 1,265 homes, destroyed hospitals, schools, churches; + 300 killed. |
| 8 | 1/1/1923 | Rosewood, Florida | A married white woman claimed to have been beaten by an unknown Black man. The posse carried out lynchings and burned the town to the ground. |
| 9 | 12/29/1923 | Catcher, Arkansas | Three Kemetic (Black) men were falsely accused of raping and killing a White woman. Two were executed, and one got Life in Prison. 40 Kemetic American families were asked to remove themselves from the town. |

Source: Zinn Education Projects' Massacres in U.S. History https://www.zinnedproject.org/collection/massacre s- us/

These simultaneous events occurred within the emergence of Garvey into the U.S. after World War I, and his phenomenal national organizing strategy reinforced the mutual and simultaneous growth of Kemetic towns that were established before World War I. They were not isolated and didn't occur in a vacuum. These major communities and others were creatively established with a local unified purpose, exemplified self-determination, unity, and cooperative economics. Similarly, residents of Tulsa and Rosewood had already established businesses, churches to instill their faith, and schools for the education of the young.

We are not responding to, reacting to, or being put on the defensive in discussions or accusations of "reverse racism", or currently being labeled as "Black Identity Extremists' (B.I.E's). Our focus is "Community Well-Being." We are creating collective "Self-Help" activities to improve our lives and create personal, physical, and spiritual abundance for Our-Selves, Our Families, and Our Communities."

Contemporary Race Massacres and Lynchings

## Table 13: Contemporary Race Massacres

|   | DATE | MASSACRE | LOCATION |
|---|---|---|---|
| 1 | 5/13/1985 | Philadelphia, Pennsylvania | Police bombed the home of the MOVE Back to Nature Organization, killing 11, leaving 250 persons homeless from the bomb destruction of the neighborhood. |
| 2 | 6/17/2015 | Charleston, South Carolina | Emanuel African Methodist Episcopal Church Massacre. Nine killed during a Bible Study, including the Sr. Pastor and State Senator Clements C. Pinckney. Murdered by 21-year-old Dylan Roof, white, allowed to join in prayer. |
| 3 | 8/25/2020 | Kenosha, Wisconsin | Kyle Rittenhouse, white, age 17, shot three demonstrators and wounded two while exposing an assault-style rifle, not apprehended, in front of police who did not intervene to protect the unarmed Black Lives Matter marchers. |
| 4 | 8/24/2020 | Kenosha, Wisconsin | Kemetic Jacob Blake, 29 years, was shot several times at point-blank range in front of his three young sons. Blake is now completely paralyzed as a result of the incident. This incident was the reason for the Black Lives Matter march mentioned above. |

The previous events were met with individual lynching, killing and property destruction, all of which exemplify a massive "knee in the neck" of Kemetic progress from Reconstruction even beyond Civil Rights and Black Power. White massacres against Kemetic American People have never stopped. Lynching and other atrocities have never stopped.

It is no wonder that white conservatives of the "Christian Right" are seeking to erase these heinous events from history so that their descendants would never know the truth. Sure, they would feel bad! Not towards other Blacks; their guilt and shame would be directed at their own ancestors. Search Alligator bait[17] – evidence of the lowest of the low! How dare they!

https://www.ferris.edu/HTMLS/news/jimcrow/question/2013/may.htm/Jim-Crow-Museum

### Always in Season Film Documents the History of Lynching

Amy Goodman, Host of Public Radio Syndicate Democracy Now, June 22, 2020, interviewed Ms. Jacqueline Olive, Independent Film Maker and Director of Always in Season, and discussed the documentary examining the history of lynchings in the United States. Always in Season premiered on February 24, 2020.

Olive states, "There's a CDC report that I've been looking at that says that there have been 79 unsolved hangings of Blacks and that they've all been males, in this report, 79 hangings that are unsolved between 2000 and 2016."

Ms. Olive goes on to mention Historic Lynching Terrorism, an upsurge in response to Barak Obama's first campaign and people being threatened with nooses or symbols of nooses; how Black lives are threatened and minimized, especially since former U.S. President Trump's lack of responsible leadership when he implied that Violence was OK; and how the present outcries are out of a

---

17      Hughes, F. (n.d.). Alligator Bait. Jim Crow Museum. https://jimcrowmuseum.ferris.edu/question/2013/may.htm/Jim-Crow-Museum

sense of emergency, given the context of this history vs. claims that the recent hangings were all cases of suicide.

To fully experience this interview, please visit:

Five Black & Brown Men Have Been Recently Found Hanged in Public. Were Some of Them Lynched? https://www.democracynow.org/2020/6/22/us_public_hangings_lynching_history

I must assert my reaction to this! Come on, Dudes! There is no way that 79 Brothers would kill themselves. Brothers don't go down like that! All by themselves, find a rope long enough to go around a tree, tie it in a noose, find some boxes or chair to stand on, then kick the stand while holding on to the noose and go belly up! I don't think so! 79 scattered over 16 years in different cities or counties between 2000 and 2016? The same M-O of suicide? Give me a Break!!!

## Economic Development Efforts

President Franklin D. Roosevelt created the first relief program since the Freedmen's Bureau due to the economic depression of the 1930s. The National Industrial Recovery Act put money into the hands of consumers to boost the strength of the economy. The Works Progress Administration (WPA) provided economic development by bringing together capital and labor into cooperative action for the national benefit.

> "Roosevelt used the rhetoric of self-help and full employment to provide the illusion that the programs were designed to help the poor. His actual sympathies were in the interest of crisis business conditions and labor discontent." (Berndt, 29)

In his critique of the Community Development Corporation and urban policy, Berndt concluded, "The fact is that the chronic unemployed, which included most Black people, remained unemployed until World War II when they enlisted in the service or were hired to replace someone who had gone into the service." These events mark the rise of the social welfare movement and its subsequent public policies regarding the poor.

We must now decide how to use self-help to actualize what we need to do to Save-Our-Selves. This is an open-ended discussion. Everyone has something to contribute from their perspective. Individually, I can ask each person to identify a most pressing need or objective. Then, put those individuals in a group to develop a plan for reaching that goal. Subject matter experts who know about that topic or have worked in that arena are now strategically changing the rules of the contest. We are changers in the game of life, those who have experienced insight into each objective.

Our communities have the same structure everywhere. There are a few large and middle-sized churches and many small churches. Mostly, women and children attend church; generally, men do not. By the way, another reality–many church organizations signed off political activity since the Civil Rights Movement–when they received huge construction grants for expansion.

We have fewer thriving businesses in our communities. Most shopping centers and malls exist beyond the county line and not in the inner city. We take our money out to them so their businesses prosper.

Many bus or public transport lines bypass inner-city neighborhoods, preventing low-income residents who don't have cars from accessing places of employment. Residents in inner city communities have had to adapt their lives to contend with Interstate highways that have cut through thriving Kemetic communities, setting up geographic barriers to community cohesiveness.

Over the past 30 years, Community Development Corporations (CDCs) have not significantly improved the conditions of the residents they were established to serve. They should have used their political savvy, clout, longevity and credibility to induce social change for the Kemetic residents they were "established" to serve. CDCs should have developed solutions that would galvanize the many and varied talents within and without the community to benefit and respond to the needs of their original Kemetic residents.

This is a perfect example of disestablishment! Most CDCs were on the profit motive and were created to emphasize venture development. It was meant to be a partnership between the community, the government (the funding source for the CDC) and the private sector. The CDC has altered its focus from serving the target population because the anti-poverty priorities were against profit-making objectives. Berndt's analysis holds true today 42 years later, "CDC's future will be toward more outside non-resident participation; employment of fewer residents, and a greater exploitative role." (Berndt, 138)

Look at us now. Most whites have forsaken their "flight" and want to live in inner city neighborhoods. Ethnic manipulation in New York City and other urban areas in the U.S. shows evidence that gentrification is well entrenched. For example, what was once a thriving banquet hall became a Scottish Community Center in Bedford-Stuyvesant. Others from war-torn Eastern Europe have migrated into Oceanhill-Brownsville. Living in the "ghetto" for them is safer than living in a war zone. All of the infill housing was geared for other than the original community residents who were never targeted for job training or employment. The Local Community Development Corporations and their corresponding Community Planning Boards in Central Brooklyn allowed and even facilitated these events.

Community Development Corporations are politically linked to the elected Officials of the day and have become their community conduit for resources. Federal and State funding projects are approved and promulgated through their offices. Voting patterns are changing as more and more new residents will vote for others, and those who have assisted in the disenfranchisement of local Kemetic residents as Elected Officials will become outvoted and disenfranchised themselves, lacking a voter base.

Crooked politicians have done no good for the community residents who voted them into office. Maybe they got caught in a "set-up" to remove them from office. It's a royal mess! Another travesty! S-O-S! How can we Save-Our-Selves?

As recently as 2017, there is the case of John Sampson, the former New York State Senate Democratic leader, District 19, in southeastern Brooklyn. He formerly served as Chairman of the Senate Judiciary and Senate Health Committees. Sampson was sentenced to concurrent five years for embezzlement of public funds. This leads to another major concern: Redistricting – the reason political and community development fell apart in Central Brooklyn. Check out the "Brooklyn Waffle.[18]"

## The Brooklyn Waffle

State Senate District 19 is located in southeastern Brooklyn, including some or all of the neighborhoods of Canarsie, East New York, Brownsville, Mill Basin, Sheepshead Bay, Bergen Beach, Marine Park, Flatlands, and Ocean Hill. The district overlaps with New York's 7th, 8th, 9th, and 11th congressional districts, and with the 41st, 42nd, 45th, 54th, 55th, 58th, 59th, and 60th districts of the New York State Assembly[19].

These overlaps of Election Districts were designed to prevent local community development by disallowing plans for new projects. Throughout the 1990s, I was a resident of Oceanhill-Brownsville and a member of the East Fulton Street Redevelopment Corporation – also known as The East Fulton Street Group, Executive Director, the late Rev. James H. Daniel, Jr.

We presented development projects and were sent from one Community Planning Committee or politician to another and were told, "That does not fit our plan." When we inquired about the plan, they responded, "It's still in the planning stage, and we're not ready to make it public."

---

18    Former State Senator Pleads Guilty to Two Counts of Embezzlement, NY1 News, Spectrum News Staff, November 2, 2018: https://ny1.com/nyc/all-boroughs/news/2018/11/02/former-state-senator-sampson-pleads-guilty-to-embezzlement
19    New York State Senate, John L. Sampson (D): https://www.nysenate.gov/senators/john-l-sampson

A 30-year retrospective reveals that all of Central Brooklyn was slated for funding "In Fill" housing in the vacant lots, and business development became available for new immigrants supported with publicly and privately funded resources–Also Known As– Gentrification. Local residents were not included in the plans.

## Community Self-Help

The 2020 Presidential Election Year required nationwide Redistricting. Solutions Specialists should have demanded that land resource allocations include local residents to reach a consensus and ensure a plan to benefit local communities for the next decade. This also coincided with the 2020 Census counts. In planning for Census 2030, solutions specialists should ensure that a clear direct line of influence and authority is enforced in their geographic areas. In New York City, this includes Police Precincts, Community School Boards, Community Planning Boards, and all Election District boundaries.

There is no need for a State Senatorial District to overlap four Congressional Districts, eight State Assembly Districts, and ten neighborhoods. Their constituencies are clearly not the voters. Private interest groups and organized communities "pull the shots." We can change this!

Let us collectively transform these false visions into realities of truth. The Kemetic American population totaled a l m o s t 90 million according to the 2020 U.S. Census. Poverty for descendants of Kemet is nothing but a smoke screen. On February 1, 2022, Frank Holland, in "Equity and Opportunity," CNBC announced that Black spending power in 2021 reached $1.6 Trillion, but our net worth fell by 14%. "Net worth is the value of the assets a person or corporation owns; minus the liabilities they owe.[20]"

Frank Holland advises people that home ownership is a good way to increase assets. One wonders whether the 14% decline is

---

20    Ganti, A. (2023, March 9). Net Worth: What It Is and How to Calculate It. Investopedia. https://www.investopedia.com/terms/n/networth.asp

related to the rise in foreclosures. So far, I have no stats on this relationship; further research is required.

The overall U.S. population is 663,394,825. Urban dwellers represent 82.8% of the total U.S. population. Kemetic descendants in America total 89,922,562 (almost 90 million.) We continue to make up 13.5% of the U.S. population.

See Table 14: Total U.S. Population Estimates by Race.

**Table 14: total united states population estimates by race (2022)**

| RACE | POPULATION |
| --- | --- |
| American Indian or Alaska Native | 8,690,240 |
| Asian | 40,499,833 |
| Black or African American | 89,922,562 |
| Native Hawaiian or Other Pacific Islander | 1,713,340 |
| White | 503,203,564 |
| More than One Race | 19,365,286 |
| TOTAL | 663,394,825 |

Note: Estimates for 2020-2021 are single-race Vintage 2021 postcensal (after census) estimates of the July 1 resident population. These estimates were prepared and released by the U.S. Census Bureau on June 30, 2022.

Source: https://wonder.cdc.gov/controller/datarequest/D184

Poverty is a subconscious code the media puts out there to make us believe in our own deprivation. This is a post Covid-19 Quarantine reality, and this assessment can assist us in re-establishing our priorities. It may incorporate the current national objectives for the Reparations Agenda.

On October 27, 2020, Human Rights Watch identified ten key issues in 2021 as domestic priorities for the next Presidential Administration, no matter who wins the election. One of the issues identified as requiring immediate attention is responding to the need for Reparations.

"Reparations: Victims of serious human rights violations, including acts of racial discrimination, have a right to an effective remedy, which includes reparations for past harms. These victims include Black communities that still endure systemic discrimination rooted in the U.S. history of slavery. The next administration should call on Congress to pass House Resolution (HR) 40, which would establish a commission to investigate the impacts of slavery and subsequent racist laws and policies that contribute to present-day discrimination, and direct proposals for reparations to Congress, including financial and other redress. If Congress does not pass HR 40 within the first 100 days, the executive order."

https://www.hrw.org/news/2020/10/27/human-rights-watch-2021-domestic-transition-priorities-next-us-administration

In the case of Jamaica Village, Southeast, Queens County, the subsequent racist laws and new immigrant preferential policies have contributed to present-day housing and job discrimination. As mentioned in Chapter 5: Ethnic Manipulation, there are an estimated 17,537 Distressed Families due to bank foreclosures, pre-foreclosures, short sales, and Sheriff sales in the 19 square miles that make up Jamaica, Southeast Queens. Also, related education deficits in Jamaica are the underachieving test scores even after years of receiving Title I status. The politically focused economic agenda has now shifted from community to regional development.

### Jamaica Downtown Revitalization Initiative (DRI)

https://www.ny.gov/sites/ny.gov/files/atoms/files/Jamaica_DRI_Plan.pdf

On July 12, 2017, Governor Andrew Cuomo announced that Jamaica, Queens, received $10 million for Downtown Revitalization. The research I conducted on this project revealed that despite the wonderful structural and technological improvements, high-speed broadband, restaurant development, hotels, "low" income new housing, murals and open spaces --- there was extremely little allocated for the economic development of the majority of African American individuals and families in the greater Jamaica area.

The DRI Planned to: *"Expand career opportunities and strengthen career pathways. DRI investments should ensure that revitalization benefits those currently living downtown by giving them skills they need to succeed in growing industries and providing avenues for local entrepreneurs to build their businesses and create jobs"* (14).

Another goal was to: *"Increase quality jobs: Establish a working group with local workforce providers, employers, and local academic institutions to identify opportunities to provide stronger, industry-linked skills training and workforce development programs that align with the City's Career Pathways framework."*

The NYC Career Pathways programs are operated by Maximus: *The NYC Career Pathways programs, operated by ("Knee in Our Necks") Maximus, are dedicated to empowering you to succeed in the career of your choice. We offer a broad range of services to support your efforts, including access to vocational and educational trainings, internships, career coaching, job matching, life-skills coaching, self-assessments, and case management. NYC Career Pathways Programs are currently operating in Harlem, The Bronx and Staten Island.*

Searching Maximus, Inc. reveals Maximus Inc., trademarked as MAXIMUS, is an American outsourcing company that provides business process services to government health and human services agencies in the United States, Australia, Canada, Saudi Arabia and the United Kingdom. Maximus focuses on administering government-sponsored programs, such as Medicaid, the Children's Health Insurance Program (CHIP), health care reform, welfare-to-work, Medicare, child support enforcement, and other government programs. The company is based in Reston, Virginia, has 34,300 employees and a reported annual revenue of $3.46 billion in fiscal year 2020.

This funding for the delivery of services to outside vendors is why there are limited numbers of locally funded providers for social service programs with local links to community realities or knowledge of neighborhood nuances. It also reinforces the requirement for professional certification of workers in non-profit organizations.

Our politicians are beginning to lose their regulatory functions of oversight of publicly funded services if there are no public services to provide to their base constituents. The vendors have less of a legal obligation to protect voters from their unethical practices, and the recipients go through a circular maze because the system is designed to satisfy only a small percentage of the people.

Solutions Specialists for Self-Help nationwide should investigate as to whether Maximus has a role and function in your region. Check whether Maximus provides similar services in your states, counties, or cities. Search to find out whether Maximus is operating in your community. Are they included in a development plan in your region?

It is important for families and communities to work together to bring in Senior Centers, Community Centers for Families, Stipend Education for Job Training and Career Preparation at local colleges to provide targeted technical training and expanded opportunities to bring about economically thriving communities established for ourselves by ourselves.

Please read my detailed "Assessment of the Jamaica Downtown Revitalization Initiative as part of the Jamaica Regional Plan" from the perspective of a Cultural Consultant-Community Scholar on the Frontline, The People's Professor.

Feel free to visit my website: https://www.SaveOurSelves.me

In 2022, local New York City Republicans were successfully represented by the Public Interest Legal Foundation in a federal lawsuit against the ratification of a proposed law introduced by Kemetic Mayor Eric Adams. The proposed local law would have allowed more than 800,000 non-citizens to vote in local New York City elections. They contended that the law was motivated by racially discriminatory intent, which violated the Voting Rights Act. There are also huge recent immigrant populations in Brooklyn and The Bronx. "It was the explicit intent of the Law's sponsors to increase the voting strength of certain racial subgroups while simultaneously decreasing the voting strength of other racial subgroups.[21]"

Reminder: This internal microscopic focus on Queens can give you a wider macroscopic view of your own county, parish, borough, or city. It's easy to find these statistical relationships when you go to https://zipdatamaps.com/. Enter your zip code, scroll down, and you can find key information about any zip code in the United States.

### Solutions Specialists: Tacticians for Self-Actualization

Wherever we are, in the entire U.S.A., local Solutions Specialists as tacticians for Self-Help are emerging. They will increasingly morph into teams of individuals who can map out all elements in play and lead the rest of us in a prioritized list of activities to address the resolution of our urgent needs. Solutions Specialists can number one person and go up to hundreds, even thousands, nationwide. Solutions Specialists must be fair, objective, and committed to interacting with all community members and groups. Begin to ask intelligent questions. Strive to arrive at and seek nothing less than infallible truth and realize infinite possibilities as we change our vision and manifest the positive results we seek.

Potential power is measured in numbers. The key to our value is our participation in the decision-making process. Solutions Specialists should plan meetings that draw people out and allow them to speak for themselves. Do not fall into the trap of ethnic favoritism and manipulation. Do not try to justify or apologize for accusations of reverse racism.

---

21  Gonan, Y. (2022, August 30). Conservatives' Federal Case Challenges Immigrant Voting — Using Ex-Council Members' Own Words. The City.

The most natural ingredients for developing the best possible resources in a community are the collective millions of thoughts within the brain power of the people themselves. A community improves as it becomes more heterogeneous, incorporating more cultural and ethnic traditions and developing the skills and confidence to solve our own problems.

Solutions Specialists for Self-Help should be involved with local and regional planning. They should come to a consensus on long and short-range goals. During the 2020 Presidential Election cycle and coinciding with preparation for the 2020 Census, Solutions Specialists had a prime opportunity to demand that land resource allocations could include local residents among the decision-makers. The goal would have been to arrive at consensus ensuring a plan benefiting local communities for the next decade. Solutions Specialists ensure that a clear direct line of influence and authority is enforced in their geographic areas. In New York City, this includes Police Precincts, Community School Boards, and Community Planning Boards. I invite the reader to research the jurisdictional boundaries in their own community.

Solutions Specialists for Self-Help should be involved with planning. They should come to a consensus on long and short-range goals. Organizational linking and person-to-person networking can be set up on social media to reach each community member and expand numbers. Solutions Specialists should encourage all groups who express a desire to work with one another on a series of defined tasks that would bring the master objective to completion. We must stop identifying with those who oppress us and reject their values and ways of thinking and living. By taking pride in ourselves, we can eliminate the self and community destructiveness that has impacted our self-help efforts in the past.

A thriving community can be the first goal of the Solutions Specialists for Self-help. Concerns might consider the interest of the welfare recipient, the unemployed, the shelter compromised, and those recently released from prison. "A chain is only as strong as its weakest link." Community consumer cooperatives may be a final alternative to community exploitation by other ethnic groups and high prices for poor-quality merchandise. Let us cultivate trust and join or form our own credit unions to manifest specific goals for home and/or community improvement. Communal living may solve the problem of high rents and poor housing.

Solutions Specialists realize that institution building is the most important long-term plan. They now include younger generations in activities that are required to remain in place to keep the plan going. Allow our youth to accompany us and share their opinions while we develop future plans. Seek advice from Elder Family Members and Community Leaders.

As Solutions Specialists, we view ourselves as the descendants of Kemet, the ancient continent and nation of people from whence all others have come. Planners can follow through with clear objectives for community collectivity to emerge. Solutions Specialists will collaborate and plan with community members on strategies to collectively address crime in our neighborhoods.

If, as mentioned previously, crime has decreased in your community, then conducting a serious critical analysis of education at all levels, from pre-kindergarten to Post Graduate College, would be a good idea. York College, City University of New York is right here in Jamaica, Queens. Find out the resources they may provide for local development. Immigrant ethnic groups and outside developers have already taken advantage of the public resources for urban planning available at York College. Together, yes, we can!

The cultural arts may play a significant role in reaching the mass public. Artists can play a significant role in reaching the mass public to promote goals that are decided by consensus of the constituencies within Social Solutions Groups. This would mutually help artists become popularized by those who can locally support a mini-local entertainment industry. Once performing and visual artists collaborate on their own behalf, they will command a greater audience. When we form a successful evidence-based methodology for Community Self-Help, the model can be taken to other urban areas nationally and globally to be used accordingly by Solutions Specialists everywhere.

Take, for instance, the nations on the Kemetic continent, each with its own unique cultural characteristics. Many are vying for development aid, and those whose politics are the correct "flavor of the day" receive it on a short-term basis at most. Like the inner cities, aid cannot possibly go to everyone. This creates an atmosphere of competition, distrust, suspicion, political compromise, and animosity between entities. We should be planning and strategizing together for the better good of all.

Human resources–people working together-are our most valuable asset. Let us start thinking globally and locally simultaneously. Let us use that which is available to us in computer software to develop local databases of retired people with valuable skills and knowledge to share. Another database should identify home improvement needs such as electronics, plumbing, roofing, carpentry, computer repair and programming, home repair, green energy, and more.

Identify those willing to take in an apprentice or two and teach critical skills. Maximize social media, then meet in person to lay out these action plans. Every six months, assess how the plan is doing and readjust the strategy to stay on target with the objective. Then, create another objective and follow that to its completion. Include the presence of our children to work with us to provide and give their insight for achieving each objective.

# SOURCES

*The community development corporation and urban policy.*
Berndt, H.E., (1977). Greenwood Press.

*African-American studies for the adult basic reader.*
Harris, V.L. (1986). MAC/AEA Literacy Project: City University of New York.

*"Marcus Garvey: Father of African Nationalism,"*
Harris, V.L. (February, 1987). CLASS Magazine: New York.

*"Toward a theory of community development."*
Harris, V.L. (1982). Unpublished.

*Garvey and Garveyism.*
Garvey, A.J. (1963)

https://www.SaveOurSelves.me

# CHAPTER NINE

## *Activating Solutions*

- We begin with a review of activism during Civil Rights and Black Power – and present a huge caution.
- Character assassinations are directed at Kemetic millionaires with social influence and credibility.
- Economic channels of control and manipulation are being set up as blockades to clog lines of support for efforts toward the social advancement of Kemetic Americans in a futile attempt to maintain the status quo.
- Beware of Agents set up to internally destroy new groups and organizations that have emerged since the "Occupy" and "Black Lives Matter" movements.
- Global, national, and local economic and social relationships are changing.
- Immediately, from this day forward, right now, at each of our individual and collective circumstances, we can operate as PROSUMERS!
- Simultaneously, we can be social catalysts for the greater good while ensuring self-directed activities;
- Maximizing our energies as we Save-Our-Selves One-by-One and All Together.

In the Kemetic principle of Sankofa, we must return to our past to go forward with informed decisions while activating long-term solutions for the greater good. Since the arrival of Kemetic people on America's shores, Kemetic descendants have been forced to react to stereotypes and prejudices of the dominant society. Social beliefs were put into law to defend the economics of free labor and low-wage exploitation. Kemetic descendants have been forced to adjust to open hostility coming from society. Our socialization involved three coping methods: resistance, avoidance or accepting our inferior status.

Avoidance involves identifying with the dominant population and believing that "white adjacent" makes one "safe." Kemetics who believe that class/caste identity by those of higher income in the attempt to avoid prejudice and discrimination by isolating themselves from those with lower income. Communities in urban areas continue to be segregated, which helped minimize interracial interaction between white and black communities. There was also a massive migration to northern cities from overt discrimination practiced in the South.

These social psychological behaviors exist to this day. Inner-directed aggression, apathetic acceptance, and avoidance are behavioral patterns that act out negative evaluations of self. The recent police killings, massacres, and lynchings of unarmed Kemetic men and women have fueled resistance in various social movements and organized group pressure to escape from or improve our status.

The Kemetic American Social Movements of the 1960s and 70s involved the developmental non-violent stages of Civil Rights, leading to the more aggressive Black Power movement. This can be compared by some to the Stages of Change Theory, moving from pre-thinking to thinking, planning, action, and maintaining our lifestyles.

Our people became complacent, believing we had "made it." We now witness more aggressive racist actions codified by legislative laws and administrative regulatory requirements. Kemetic regression occurs when we think we have achieved vital goals and become too comfortable, not understanding that positive change or progress is dynamic and must be maintained and nurtured with consistent action and attention.

A retrospective view of the organized social movements of the late 1960s to mid-1970s shows that regression occurred when certain improvements brought about a sense of complacency, resulting in limited continued support for status-quo community programs. The National Action Network (NAN), founded in 1991 and led by Rev. Al Sharpton, continues to organize locally and nationally, focusing on key issues.

NAN has maintained local and national influence due to their ability to exhibit institutional credibility conferred by the external establishment and longevity earned by the leadership. It is essential, at this point, to caution new leadership of the militant masses that those in White America who want to maintain the status quo are likely to send individuals who orchestrate scenarios that create in-group dissent and result in mistrust among social activists who are now the front runners in the struggle.

The kinetic reality of organization renewal can be implemented to ensure that institutionalized established Civil Rights organizations can train and nurture Solutions Specialists to conduct workshops to address community needs relevant to the 21st Century. Every one of us has a role in this change process.

The National Association of Kawaida Organizations (NAKO) is celebrating 50 years of organizing and development under the leadership of Dr. Maulana Karenga. NAKO popularized the National and Global celebration of Kwanzaa by establishing strong nationwide coalitions, forming a Black Federation with Independent Black Schools and other organizations, and convening Black Power Conferences. The Kwanzaa Principles were developed from Kawaida as moral ideals of how we engage with one another.

Kwanzaa was formed to celebrate Kemetic American culture and history. Kemetic descendants are encouraged to practice the Nguzo Saba or 7 Principles as we actualize activities to Save-Our-Selves:

- Unity – Umoja
- Self-Determination – Kujichagulia
- Collective Work and Responsibility – Ujima

- Cooperative Economics – Ujamaa
- Purpose – Nia
- Creativity – Kuumba
- Faith – Imani

Kwanzaa is the celebration of Family, Community, and Culture.

NAKO began as an organization that created a national youth movement by planning Black Power Conferences organized by local groups. NAKO conducted National Symposia on "Culture and Community," presenting current events from a Kawaida perspective.

As a guest on the 11-7-2020 podcast of the Harlem News Network, Dr. Karenga elaborated on how he conceptualized Kawaida as a philosophy. He sought to put a Kemetic-African worldview into the practice of living our lives and taking the best ideas in the world. He expounded on Kawaida as a moral ideal, critically examining how we engage with strangers and each other. Kawaida grounds teachings on ethical values related to our environment. Dr. Karenga says, "There is no culture richer than ours, and as we struggle to be and free ourselves, we should share work and wealth and think revolution as we demand reform." He encourages us to build for eternity so we can live for eternity.

Social Solutions leaders and managers in established organizations can initiate, support, and reinforce change by updating their objectives and revising internal operations. They are encouraged to redesign their activities using "prosumer" strategies outlined in the last section of this chapter. Each one of us has a role in this change process. Collectively, we are compelled to manage better the $1.6 Trillion Kemetic Americans generate annually in the United States economy. This figure is impacted by the decline in our net worth due to the nationwide economic disparities in housing and education we are presently experiencing. We must implement strategies to redirect our spending, using prosumer economics creatively.

An important factor in the Civil Rights Movement was the amount and quality of leaders who served as referents for the people. Mass media and currently social media for the "Black Lives Matter" movement with slogans of "Hands Up: Don't Shoot" and "I Can't Breathe" as organized nonviolent marches are playing important roles in bringing the protests to national and international prominence.

Both movements, then and now, had participants who practiced non-violent actions, resulting in an overwhelming sense of individual and group dignity, objectivity, effectiveness and intrinsic worth. Incidents of white establishment aggression towards Kemetic descendants are now occurring at an unprecedented rate in the United States. They are creating every public means reinforced by legal precedents to kill our men, women, girls, and boys and receive rewards for their cowardly acts of aggression.

Since April 12, 2015, the death of 25-year-old Freddie Gray in police custody in Baltimore, Maryland, sparked ongoing demonstrations for "self-determination by any means necessary." This act took place in the face of extreme economic deprivation in their environment. Baltimoreans were actively and aggressively participating in their call for community self-defense. Soon after the killing of Freddie Gray, on June 17, 2015, a 22-year-old white male was welcomed into a prayer meeting at the Emanuel AME Church in Charleston, South Carolina, where he opened fire, killing nine parishioners of Kemetic descent.

Historical development of the Civil Rights Movement shows us that the time span went from 1954 with Brown vs. the Board of Education Topeka, where segregated schools were outlawed, leading to the Montgomery, Alabama bus boycott in 1955, to the March on Washington in 1965 and the assassination of Martin Luther King, Jr. in 1968.

"Black Power" was introduced as a slogan on May 29, 1966, in a speech at Howard University by the Late Harlem Congressman Adam Clayton Powell, Jr., who said, "Blacks should demand basic human rights, seek black power, and build black institutions." The Black Panthers became nationally prominent in 1967.

Today, it is important for us to be aware of the persuasive techniques that caused our show of unity and solidarity to be short-lived. The process of change was stopped by another type of persuasive communication, activated by the physical and character assassination of our leaders. Character assassination occurs when rumor or hearsay is sent throughout the community externally via the media, and internally folks can "hear it through the grapevine."

The newly established target beliefs of "Black Power," which brought about the national group solidarity, were manipulated from outside to inside by inter and intra-organizational conflict. The best example would be the bitter infighting between the US Organization and the Black Panther Party in California. The positive role of unity was transformed into fighting, mistrust, and bickering.

The active role of the Federal Bureau of Investigation Counterintelligence Program and its in-group manipulation is now public knowledge. Nelson Blackstock (1975: 84) wrote *Cointelpro: The FBI's Secret War on Political Freedom*. His research revealed, "Targets of the Federal Bureau of Investigation's (FBI's) systematic sabotage of the Black movement included: Dr. Martin Luther King, Jr., the Nation of Islam, Rev. Ralph Abernathy's Poor People's Campaign, Stokeley Carmichael, and the Black Panther Party, the NAACP and the Committee to Aid the Monroe Defendants, Black members of the Socialist Worker's Party and others."

In order to be labeled a KBE or Key Black Extremist, an individual needed to be "extremely active and most vocal in opposition to racial discrimination." In 1970, the FBI warranted intensified coverage to bring to bear the total capabilities of the Bureau on investigations of these individuals. "We should cover every facet of their activities, future plans, weaknesses, strengths, and personal lives to neutralize the effectiveness of each KBE. The finances, travel, utterances, and possible violations of Federal and local laws of these individuals should receive the closest investigative and supervisory attention" (Blackstock, 87).

The term KBE did not require that an individual actually hold an official position in an organization, but was to include others of equal importance because of their influence as Black "extremists." Between 1967 and 1971, there was an awakening of Black consciousness. Documents reveal that uppermost in the minds of J. Edgar Hoover, Director of the FBI, and his associates were their desire to trammel the efforts of Black organizations to win followers (Blackstock, 90).

The anti-poverty programs gave temporary incentive rewards in salaries and program development to those who became community leaders. Administrative jobs that controlled certain community programs increased individual prestige and were primarily obtained by those with middle-class status. Welfare payments were increased for people experiencing poverty.

Increased amounts of LSD, cannabis, heroin, cocaine, and other hard drugs were introduced into all income levels of the Kemetic community. This brought about individual euphoric pleasure and pacification, so there was no incentive to strive for gratification via societal achievement. Persons became complacent and selfishly individualistic. Black-on-Black crime became the mode for supporting the drug culture. This caused suspicion and mistrust to increase and become prevalent in Kemetic communities. Anti-drug laws began to be enforced. It is important to note that before approximately 1967, the incarcerated population in the United States was approximately 98% white.

Young leaders and activists of today should be mindful that there is no such thing as privacy. Follow the advice of Prophet Elijah Mohammed, peace be unto him, and don't give the authorities any criminal reason to arrest you and take you into custody. Crime and civil disobedience are two different acts.

The criminal element actually represents a small percentage of our overall population. The victims are the silent and self-isolated majority, numbering 89.9 million. The first object of the influence attempt should be directed at this community element, getting us to trust one another. This attention would likely change community members' basic beliefs about each other.

It is not necessary to see Kemetic community characteristics targeted for influence as being that of pre-1960. We have just about gone full cycle out of those social psychological behaviors of powerlessness and apathy. Our self-esteem has been reinforced from becoming Black and Proud – to being focused on the objective of self-actualization. What needs to be done is to reaffirm community characteristics prior to the massive individual and group manipulation in the early 1970s.

This is the point of reference from which we step into a new era in economic and cultural development as we target objectives for collective mass influence. Again, we are not responding, reacting to, or being put on the defensive in discussions or accusations of "reverse racism," or currently, being labeled as "Black Identity Extremists." Our focus is "Community Well-Being." Solutions Specialists are creating "Self-Help" activities to improve our lives and create personal, physical, and spiritual abundance for Our Selves, Our Families, and Our Communities.

## From Being Consumers to Becoming Prosumers

Beginning in 1970 and approximately each decade since, Alvin Toffler (1928-2016) and his wife, Heidi Toffler, examined the political, economic, and social constantly changing individual, local, national and global trends. Their books were published as *Future Shock* (1970); *The Third Wave: The Classic Study of Tomorrow* (1980); and *Power Shift: Knowledge, Wealth, and Violence at the Edge of the 21st Century* (1990). Among other intermittent books were *War and Anti-War* (1993) and *Creating a New Civilization* (1994) as events continued to accelerate political, economic, cultural, and social trends worldwide.

In 2006 came another seminal and revealing book, *Revolutionary Wealth: How It Will Be Created and How It Will Change Our Lives*. They speak of combining the visible and hidden economies, which combine into a wealth creation system. Upon bringing together the two, "the money system is going to expand dramatically. But what we do *without money* will have a bigger and bigger impact on what we do *with* money. Prosumers are the unsung heroes of the economy to come." (Toffler, A&H, 179) Let us explore this!

An intellectual interpretation of their overall analyses regarding the role of descendants of Kemet living in America is inappropriate in this writing. So, I will "cut to the chase."

We are 89.9 million strong. We currently generate $1.6 Trillion of wealth into the American system. The public education system is not meeting the needs of many of our children. Many low-income children are being groomed for incarceration and free labor for the Prison Industrial Complex, commonly known as the School-to-Prison Pipeline. College is overpriced for most. Those who are unemployed are not counted in the system, yet we do all kinds of work for ourselves and each other every day. Our people are dying disproportionately in all disease areas. We purchase clothing and other items made everywhere but here, collectively feeding families in Asia, specifically China and India.

The Tofflers introduced the term "Prosumer" in *The Third Wave*, and they elaborate on it in *Revolutionary Wealth*. Essentially, it translates as "Do It Yourself." We will use our prosumer power to increase our individual, family, neighborhood, and community well-being, and it does not necessarily imply that everyone will become super rich. The goal and mutual purpose for Kemetics living in America is to manifest, reinforce, and maintain Global Economic Parity for ourselves and our progeny.

In my work as an Evaluator, I learned about Wilfredo Pareto, who conceptualized the theory that 20% of the major or worst problems an organization or community experiences are 80% of the solution to overall improvement. We now understand that high incidences of inner-city crime are a false narrative. Violent crime decreased tremendously in the last 28 years. Using this example, we can easily identify education as a major challenge in our communities, which is very often linked to illiteracy. So, let's take on education from a prosumer perspective.

It is evident in so many ways that public education has not met the needs of Kemetic children living in America. Many parents have chosen to "homeschool" their children rather than subject them to six or seven hours a day in a psychologically traumatic environment. It is possible to evolve homeschool into a Group School reality using the same online resources and develop culturally relevant, age-appropriate lessons for learning.

The Group School or Mini School could take place in a renovated abandoned building, church or collective of churches, or even our homes. Collaboratively, members of organizations can develop a database or list of retired school personnel, teachers, counselors, professionals, entrepreneurs, businessmen and women. The list will identify those willing and able to replenish their gifts in teaching young people who are teachable and parents or guardians who are open to receiving proactive counseling and advice in the interest of their children.

Take a survey of what our young people would like to know about or learn. Use social media to recruit students and adult volunteers. Each of us has knowledge and expertise we can share with others. By the time students graduate from high school, they should have acquired the discipline, mindset, and maturity to meet all challenges in the adult world.

They should be prepared for college, vocational training or possess a skill ready to produce items in a local, national, or global prosumer market. Let us join our "pulsating pineal pinecones" and put our heads together, planning and executing greater visions and realities for our families and communities.

As a Self-Help community option, the Covid-19 quarantine

and school closures have popularized alternative concepts that have already been in progress and parallel the suggested parental and community establishment of the Mini-School. National School Choice Week provides excellent examples of scenarios that can retrofit families, communities, or organizations that opt for quality education and unique learning environments for their children impacted by the quarantine.

Learning environments are described as Pandemic Pods, Learning Pods, Micro Schools, Homeschool Co-Ops, and One-Room Class Rooms. There are opportunities to develop tailored curricula determined by Parental protocols. "Whichever curriculum you choose, make sure it is well-rounded and gives students a balance between learning and enrichment activities." This Website provides State by State requirements, guidelines, and definitions determined by learning pod choice options that have continued beyond the pandemic period.

https://schoolchoiceweek.com/learning-pods/ #sectionpodcosts

The Tofflers present Linux and the availability of a free open-source computer operating system as an example of collective prosumer power. In 1991, Linux began as a brainchild of Linus Torvalds, who worked with giant computers while he was a student at Helsinki University in Finland. It took him three years to refine the code and apply it to smaller personal computers. This became the core of the Linux operating system, which he made free to the public and is now used by millions worldwide who have been able to avoid the expense of Microsoft software (Toffler, A&H, 176).

Similarly, we can take advantage of the MOOCs (Massive Open Online Courses) available on the Web. The expense of receiving undergraduate and graduate college education has become unattainable for many descendants of Kemet. Many of these courses are free or reasonably priced and taught by professors in colleges and universities worldwide. Many of the courses confer reasonably priced Certificates in various fields of professional expertise upon completing the courses.

Our micro prosumer communities need well trained and well- informed personnel to provide for our needs and teach/train our children. Search MOOC or visit: https://www.coursera.com to explore the limitless amount of information and number of certificate programs, subjects, or topics that meet our professional and knowledge enhancing needs.

The Tofflers say that in this new economy, "spending is shifting toward the services that are becoming more expensive…" and they list examples of "high-intensity fields such as health, education, media, entertainment, and financial services"(Toffler, A&H, 256). We can provide these services for ourselves and do a better job because we care for our "own" elders and children. We can heal our family members with special gifts of knowledge and health. Take a look and see what the MOOCs have to offer.

We can "coordinate centers of advanced, highly productive enterprises on the brain power of our youth" (Toffler, A&H, 304) to facilitate trade within and among each of the Big Black Cities as envisioned by Harold Cruse in the spirit of true cultural development. The Tofflers corroborate Cruse's vision as well as the vision of Kwame Nkrumah when they say, "Technology alone offers no remedy for ignorance. Political, economic, and social forces must be mobilized to educate the coming generation" (Toffler, A&H, 313).

Now let us expand our pineal pinecone perspectives in prosumer marketing. Through the years, I have been privileged to purchase unique clothing, creative art pieces, and household items since 1967 at the Kwanzaa Expos, African Street Festivals, International African Festivals, Black Expos, Atlantic Antic, and other Street Fairs that continue to take place here in Brooklyn and New York City. These markets now take place in many other urban areas all over the USA.

The market stalls create avenues of cultural ambience and are a joy to behold! Very often, my critical observation revealed that there were too many of the same product, which limits the ability of vendors to maximize intended profits. So, there is a need to diversify to a degree.

However, merchants can scale up their profits using prosumer prerogatives and expand their collective thinking using pineal pinecone brain power to benefit family members. Generally, the merchant's objective is to sell off his or her inventory at the end of the festival, and when this does not manifest, they pack up to sell in the next venue. We should take another economic view of bartering.

On the last day of the festival, consider merchant to merchant bartering. One merchant has young children and sells fashions and dresses; another merchant sells children's clothing and could use a dressy outfit for special occasions. Both have small profits from the sale of their goods to festival attendees. Keep the cash you have earned and barter your excess inventories! This is a prosumer practice for mutual benefit.

On Wall Street, they call it "International Counter Trade, which occurs between no less than 200 countries around the World annually, valued between $800 Billion and $1.2 Trillion. This reduces their currency risk and is determined by their coincidence of need" (Toffler, A&H, 282).

Barter with a purpose as opportunity permits. Don't buy clothes --- Exchange them! We can design and manufacture our own lines of clothing for the family! Exchange Skills -- among individual homeowners by developing group projects. Skills such as Electricians, Plumbers, Fashion Designers, Tailors, Auto Mechanics, Computer Technicians, Website Developers, and Roofers, etc., can also be bartered for mutual benefit. Bring on an apprentice who wants to learn and is teachable.

Adopt the practice of: "You train my Child --- I train your Child." Work together with responsibility to produce quality work, affirming a commitment to reject mediocrity in all we do. Each inner city can support at least one mini-scaled Vocational Institute in the spirit of Booker T. Washington's Tuskegee, the brainchild and birthplace of vocational education in the United States.

In our scaled-down and mutually benefiting market of almost 90 million Kemetics in America, we can establish "mini" inner-city factories concentrating key products by creating a unique industry in each of the Black Cities (the brainchild of Harold Cruse, mentioned in the "Introduction") for mutual trading purposes. Co-operative small-scale manufacturing units can be maintained for possible seasonal/rotating mixed-use, merchandising, and processing of unique products. Merchants can increase their inventories and hire workers temporarily or permanently using this shared space.

We can establish and maintain active use of Community Van Lines for "public" community transportation along avenues not supported by public systems. "Dollar Vans" have been Caribbean-influenced innovative alternative businesses that grew since the 1980 Transit strike. They are now described as the "shadow transit" lines of New York City. Check out this unique history on the interactive page in the NewYorker.com entitled, "New York's Shadow Transit.[22]" Explore how a similar innovative plan can benefit your community.

These Community Van Lines limit walking or waiting for the limited number of overcrowded buses. Maintain van use even if the city increases its fleet in direct belated competition. Remember the Montgomery, Alabama Bus Boycott! In self-determination, we continue to Support-Our-Selves.

These are just a few examples of the projects we can activate or reactivate to change our economy and cultivate our social realities by collectively working together and applying prosumer strategies. We can maintain current and develop new businesses, organizations and institutions. Our prerogative is to respect the reality of individual free will and collective choice by working with interested people.

We can plan meet-ups in our living rooms, community rooms,

---

22      New York's Shadow Transit: https://projects.newyorker.com/story/nyc-dollar-vans/

churches, and other shared spaces. There are billions of brain cells surrounding our pulsating pineal pinecones, and we can share our ideas and activate solutions that we often already conceived in our minds. Now is the time!

The universe evidences the time as we enter a new Epoch, and The Sun centering our Solar System is aligned with the center of our Milky Way Galaxy. According to the Mayan Calendar, we can anticipate 1,000 years or even more of peace on Earth. We are experiencing energies of regurgitation from those who want to maintain the old way before 1958 here in the USA. In stagnation, they react emotionally with fear, hatred, jealousy, envy, and unsure of their own futures. They are projecting mental, emotional, and physical violence upon others to cover up their own insecurities in a world that is accelerating forward without their influence.

Yes, we should vote for the candidates who are least harmful to our communities - no matter which party prevails. For us, it doesn't matter who wins! We are the only ones who can Save-Our-Selves!

It is an undisputed truth that peoples of the World have been wondering about and anticipating the eventual evidence of the awakening genius of descendants of Kemet living in America. We, the Kemetic Citizens, have witnessed first-hand the education, technology, environmental changes, and the social contradictions "of a democratic, perfect union, providing for the common defense, establishing justice, ensuring the domestic tranquility for ourselves and our posterity." We are accelerating without fear or compromise as sophisticated, non-drug influenced, problem-solving innovators collectively Saving-Our-Selves and Planet Earth from human destruction.

# SOURCES

*Cointelpro: The FBI's secret war on political freedom.*
Blackstock, Nelson. (1975). Vintage Books: New York.

*Prologue to liberation: A history of black people in America.*
Carlisle, Rodney. (1972). Appleton-Century: New York.

*Belief, attitude, intention and behavior: An introduction to theory and research.*
Fishbein, Martin. (1975). Addison-Wesley: Reading, Massachusetts.

*African origin of biological psychiatry.*
King, R.D., MD. (2010, revised). Richard D. King: Las Angeles, California.

*Racial and cultural minorities: An analysis of prejudice and discrimination.*
Simpson, G.E. & Yinger, J.M. (1965, 3rd Ed.). Harper & Row: New York.

*"The relevance of beliefs, attitudes, and intentions for an understanding of the problems associated with attempts to bring about change."*
Harris, V.L. (1983). Unpublished manuscript.

*Revolutionary Wealth.*
Toffler, A & Toffler, H. (2006). Albert A. Knopf: New York

# CHAPTER TEN

## *Social Situation Surmountable*

- First, we discover the truth about our own communities in real numbers
- We incorporate elements of development by teaching, learning, and facilitating on a mass scale
- We cultivate self-discipline by being mindful of our food and drink intake

**Together Yes, We Can**

A reliable way to document the level of distressed families in our neighborhoods is to find out the number of foreclosures within the same zip code. This list should include bank, foreclosures, pre-foreclosures, short sales and sheriff sales. If you notice a familiar address on the list, don't make an issue except to assist or support. You are looking for the total foreclosures in each zip code (postal) area. Visit and type in your zip code: https://www.foreclosurelistings.com/ This is a nationwide listing source.

Then, go to https://www.zipdatamaps.com/ to discover the key social features in your community. Make a note of your zip code area in square miles, current population, number of bank foreclosures (in the same zip code from your original search), racial majority, public school racial majority, school test performance, and unemployment rate. Scroll down to read the text and view the circle tables about populations in your zip code area.

Homeownership is a major way to build wealth. When we lose our homes or businesses due to any category of foreclosing, it reduces the status of available assets for ourselves, our families, and our descendants. "Reparations should come in the form of wealth-building opportunities that address racial disparities in education, housing, and business ownership...the nationwide call for reparations seeks to reduce the racial wealth gap and to compensate descendants of enslaved Black Americans for their labor."

The Brookings Institution supported independent research on the call for reparations. In 2020, Research Fellows Rashawn Ray and Andre Perry completed extensive research to respond to the question, "Why we need reparations for Black Americans.[23]" You can access the "Executive Summary" from the following link:

*Resist Turbulent Times - Ways to Save-Our-Selves* sought to discover the root cause or causes that impacted the social development of Kemetics living in America. It was necessary to discover events in society that blocked our growth and development since immigrant groups have been able to prosper over time.

In Chapter 7: "Cultivating Tacticians for Self-Actualization," I documented the fact that the massacres, burning down of homes, schools, churches and businesses, and lynchings have never stopped in the 160 years since the 1863 Emancipation Proclamation. Family elders went silent due to their deep-seated fear and post-traumatic reactions responding to these memories.

Ms. Ida B. Wells-Barnett (1862-1931), originally from Memphis, Tennessee, conducted a national campaign against lynching throughout her life. After more than 100 years and 200 attempts, the U.S. Senate passed the Anti- Lynching Law on March 8, 2022.

Currently, the FBI's National Crime Information Center (NCIC) database lists 424,066 missing children under 18 in 2018, the most recent year for which data is available. About 37% of those children are black, even though black children only make up about 14% of all children in the United States.

Jason Williams wrote an article, "Black People's Organs are Being Harvested and Sold on the Black Market for Millions of

---

23  Ray, R., & Perry, A. M. (2020, April 15). Why we need reparations for Black Americans. Brookings Institute. https://www.brookings.edu/articles/why-we-need-reparations-for-black-americans/

Dollars" (10-20-2020). He asks, "Why does it seem to be that the organs of melanated people are the ultimate prize? Because Black people are made of the most dominant substance in the universe, Melanin."

Although somewhat dated, the article reveals that USA Today conducted a report in 2006 that revealed, "in the 19 years between 1987 and 2006, over 16,800 individuals pursued lawsuits stating that their loved one's body parts were illegally sold for an estimated $6 million." The information was based on figures obtained from federal and local investigators, public organizations and medical universities.

This evidence of lynchings and unresolved abductions supports the fact that Kemetic Americans are compelled to hold our family members near and dear to Our-Selves with more sharing of our whereabouts. BlackNews.com 2-15-2019 reported, "as of 2014, about 64,000 Black Women and Girls have gone missing." If possible, folks are advised to travel and move about with a Buddy at all times. Keep your children under close watch for their own safety.

The actual "Eugenics Plan" for depopulating the World is in full swing. A different type of Self-Discipline is needed so that we don't help Global Planners achieve their goals. Our primary objective is to Save-Our-Selves, so we become fully conscious of the foods we eat, cut down on junk food consumption, and eat healthy as much as possible. We stop killing each other so as not to support this depopulation plan.

In International terms, "development" implies teaching, showing, facilitating, training, and more. When prefaced by political, economic, cultural and community, specific guidance is required on a mass scale. The responsibility is with each of us who knows, and we return to the now functional slogan, "Each One, Teach One," as we actualize these realities. Active participation is needed by every one of us in order for us to Save-Our-Selves. I challenge every national organization to take on a chosen task with a single objective. Once that objective is resolved, identify another goal and work with your local chapters to see improvements manifest.

This **Open-Source Proposal** is simple–not complex. Simultaneous Mass Treatments can be initiated by every national organization whose members have expertise in professional and technical fields. Each Executive Body identifies just one social issue to target. This could be from member consensus where the members strategize local solutions for the National Org's targeted social issue. Other national organizations can similarly do the same. If they identify the same social issue, they share expertise, and solutions evolve up and down the chain of their local memberships. Local memberships can also share their successes as best practices or challenges with other members or groups in various cities or counties.

There are numerous challenges to address, including
- Basic needs – food, clothing, shelter
- Nutrition insecurity
- Issues of housing insecurity/Instability/Homelessness
- Affordability of quality healthcare
- Quality education
- Homeschooling internet accessibility, computer ownership
- School-to-prison pipeline, policing – community and school
- Social isolation
- Mental health
- Exoneration and return of Kemetic American medical doctors, dentists, and pharmacy owners (maintaining family assets, licensing and certification, business development)

Another concern for attention is assisting Kemetic farmers in keeping their land, improving crops, and establishing a channel for the distribution of their products. There is no end to the focused interventions our national and local organizations can target to impact the lives of almost 90 million people. These Open-Source Solutions impact our collective ability to Save-Our-Selves.

Established community or faith-based organizations can form Social Solutions Committees, or community members can form Social Solutions Groups to address the objective to Save-Our-Selves. They can seek out retired individuals who can share their expertise with the Groups.

Retirees may be ready to teach and share their expertise if your Social Solutions Group members are open to mutually considering and following their advice. There are many retired professionals who have the spare time to provide key pointers that can guide your objectives. They possess years of expertise in Business, Financial, Education, Housing, Public Health, Urban Environment, Social Services, or Skilled Trades. After you gather your team, list the additional information you need. Conduct a mini search by interviewing elders in the community to get leads on persons who can assist you in meeting your objective. Begin with people who are familiar with you for purposes of safety and trust. Ask whether you can get their support and recommend others who might be of assistance.

Sample professional organizations may include National Black Social Workers, National Black Nurses, National Society of Black Engineers, or even your local Veterans Organization. Conduct a search for National African American Professional Organizations or Associations. There might be a local member or chapter in your city or state. The professional organization may have a Retiree's Association or member list that can connect you with volunteers interested in serving as an advisor or mentor to your project.

It is important that your Social Solutions Group is serious and interacts with the professional group or contact in a business-like manner. Be very clear on your objectives before approaching professionals willing to assist your group. Your approach may encourage or discourage their engagement with you depending on how your representative presents him or herself. Dress the part, but don't overdress – in business or business casual attire. It may be beneficial to practice using a prepared script about your Social Solutions Group and the assistance or advice you seek.

The professional organization may have or be interested in establishing an apprenticeship program. Some of your Social Solutions Group members may be interested in being trained in a specific profession or skill. Group members may be interested in becoming licensed and/or certified Nurses, Medical Assistants, Medical Technicians, Social Workers, Social Service Providers, Electricians, Plumbers, Roofers, Carpenters, Welders, or Environmental Specialists. You might be surprised to discover how quickly your Social Solutions Group can resolve your objective by following the leads of those knowledgeable about the elements of your chosen action project.

Root cause analysis is a methodology used in multiple businesses, manufacturing, and, in our case—mental healthcare—social community settings or systems that view actions related to other actions that can trigger event after event until you have a problem or multiple problems. These events negatively impact our individual, family, and community well-being.

Massacres and lynchings documented in Tables 11: Records of Race Massacres (1863-1877) and 12: Records of Race Massacres (1918-1923) document the primary root causes showing cumulative historical evidence. Massacres and lynchings impacted the second tier of ongoing attempts at self-determination in politics-voting, housing, education, business development, and/or economics.

A third tier of impacted actions has evolved into disenfranchisement, prevention of development projects, and using policies to change and twist the focus of the rules, including abortion rights, Anti-Drug Laws and Anti-Crime Laws. Media attention places blame and instills deep fear against Kemetic

Americans and people of color. The most affluent and influential Kemetic individuals are targeted with mass public character assassinations supported by undue punishment. The list goes on. The root cause of Kemetic social disenfranchisement is the non-stop massacres and lynchings in all their anti-social manifestations.

As of March 2023, in Southeast Jamaica, Queens, New York City, there were not enough jobs to support mortgages, resulting in this 19 square mile area of families enduring more than 17,537 pre-foreclosures, short sales, sheriff's sales and bank foreclosures of homes.

In addition to "targeting the root cause or causes for the effects that prevent our well-being," local and national organizations can identify the required solutions to get answers to the question of "Who? What? How many? Where? How much? It is important to note that people were not paid for their efforts in the Civil Rights or Black Power Movements. Active engagement in these "Open-Source Activities" will result in Individual, Family, and Community Well-Being in quantum leaps forward.

Kwame Nkrumah, the first President of Ghana in West Africa, connects knowledge with action in (1964) *Consciencism: Philosophy and Ideology for De- Colonization*. He believed that it was necessary to equate positive and negative action based on statistical analysis, which would determine the ways in which the actions are interrelated in any given society. Nkrumah sought to promote individual development. Based on his analysis, employment and housing for residents of Jamaica, Queens are heavily skewed as negative actions. It is important for the exact same data set to be searched for all counties in the United States to compare the differences and similarities. After the analyses are combined, we then plan our political, economic, and cultural development, making decisions based on real numbers.

The commitment of almost 90 million Kemetic descendants living in America should be to work together with people you know or people you will get to know to Save-Our-Selves. Concrete knowledge is followed by action according to the philosophy of Kwame Nkrumah.

"...so, in society every development, every progressive motion, is a resultant of unharmonious forces, a resultant, a triumph of positive action over negative action. This triumph must be accompanied by knowledge, for in the way that the process of natural evolution can be aided by human intervention based on knowledge, so...social evolution can be helped along by political intervention based upon knowledge of the laws of social development. Political action aimed at speeding up social evolution is of the nature of a catalyst..." (104)

Kwame Nkrumah suggests that societies need that catalyst because of the wastefulness of natural evolution, which could suffer the cost of massive loss of life during war or, in the case of the United States—a possible bloodbath (Code: Zombie) instigated by misinformed and misdirected elements of white supremacy extremists—resulting in unmitigated anguish among all American citizens. We are compelled to use our talents to turn the conversations into those of peace.

"Evolution speeded by scientific knowledge is prompter and represents an economy of material. In the same way, the catalysis which political action introduces into social evolution represents an economy of time, life and talent."

Multi-cultural organizations interested in sharing alternative information to bring about support that would help to dispel the negative emotions among and within the populace would make ideal collaborators with one another.

Kemetic Americans must avoid losing sight of our priority to Save-Our-Selves "One-by-One and All-Together." There is a need to take this microscopic view of Jamaica, Queens County, NYC and compare this with the economic and social status of populations throughout the mostly urban areas in each state. Local residents as Solutions Specialists can identify targeted needs and work together to strategize activities with short and long-term time frames to inform and engage each other in this crucial work. Jobs, affordable housing, and health are crucial concerns directly impacting family survival.

There are Regional Development undertakings in process, which affect all families. Collectively identify the plans and see how they impact your communities. Where there are key cities in each state, identify and share ways Solutions Specialists can collaborate on targeted needs to prioritize. States have Colleges and University systems with faculty and student bodies available to share resources to assist. Some also have Cooperative Extension mandates. All you have to do is inquire about members of student organizations and or faculty with interest in your identified priorities. The key is communication.

Strategies centered around collaborative advantage as a way of working with organizations with mutual benefit for all parties may be helpful in your approach. "Organizations are getting together to provide coordinated services such as community advice or community education to tackle social issues such as community development, drug abuse, cross-sector local economic development, or national conflicts, etc" (Huxham, 2). *Creating Collaborative Advantage* is an excellent source for directing community organizations to manifest their vision for community improvement into a reality.

> "Collaborative empowerment begins within the community and is brought to public, private, or nonprofit institutions." (p.30) The community has to be organized and endorse the collaborative plan. Community organization members need to show how they will strategize ways the invited institution can share in the community process.

In the initial stages, community members, as Solutions Specialists, are advised to have real-time discussions as they share their personal vision for community change while being open to compromise on key issues. Ideally, the community organization or statewide chapter of a national organization should do their homework, identify the focused objective, set a time frame for resolution, identify their collaboration approach, and execute a written mission plan. You may also collaborate with other local organizations who share the same goals.

We are not responding to, reacting to, or being put on the defensive in discussions or accusations of "reverse racism," or currently being labeled as "Black Identity Extremists" B.I.E.'s. Our focus is "Community Well-Being." We are creating collective "Self-Help" activities to improve our lives and create personal, physical, and spiritual abundance for our Selves, our Families, and our Communities.

This Open-Source Proposal may provide direction for Leaders or Members of Community Organizations, Associations, Groups, Faith-Based Organizations, or Think Tanks. Collectively, we can identify and execute a plan or direction for activating massive social solutions that impact us all. National organizations have the potential to engage with each other – breaking their Organization Silos.

It's important to be aware that there may be some local individuals who are members of multiple organizations that may collude with local politicians whose agendas are not congruent with the needs or interests of their community residents. This participatory Open-Source strategy can evolve into a Thriving Virtual Black Wall Street for all of us in "Real Time."

## Conclusion

All Over Everywhere Kemetic People in the United States---We Thrive! We prosper. We flourish. We are successful, especially as a result of industry, economy and good management. It is important to cultivate a higher set of values different from the dominant society. We can reinforce and improve the Fundamental Features of Family.

We can redirect our focus on Everyone's Education to facilitate economic needs and influence economic life. We will have resolved 80% of our overall objective by first targeting our most urgent need in Saving-Our-Selves. We can activate the 7 **Principles of Kwanzaa** with an increased number of Kemetics contributing to positive action and commitment to improving the quality of our work.

### Activating Abundance with a KWANZAA Foundation

On a greater scale, this self-actualization through **Self-Determination** will lead us to abundance. We will experience collective wealth in control of our **Cooperative Economics** and business development. We own our own businesses and hire our own employees. We eliminate our need for externally provided social services using our **Creativity** with the **Purpose** of taking care of our Own. We have the skills to provide Education, Health Services, Elder Care, and for our own children through Foster Care and Adoption. We develop our own industries powered by **Collective Work and Responsibility.** As a result of **Faith** in God and mutual trust, we **Save-Our-Selves**. Truly, in **Unity**, there is strength.

# AFTERWORD

Let us get this straight - We are all "Born Woke!" Generations of massacres and lynchings are implanted in our DNA from the womb to the cradle to full Adulthood and beyond to our Ancestors. So, "Anti Woke" angry political campaigns of Far-Right Republicans are blowing hot air – reacting to undo or erase or promote the heinous historical reality they created and continue to perpetrate.

We are all accelerating swiftly in a place of dynamic motion when events are rapidly evolving and occurring simultaneously --- at the same time. In March 2023, I learned about a human presence of being for Us All as Global Citizens and members of Civil Society, as defined by the United Nations. I was honored and privileged to attend, with more than 900 attendees – Global Citizens, the 2nd United Nations Permanent Forum on People of African Descent from May 31st through June 2nd 2023. The 2nd UN PF-PAD resulted in creating the provision, of support, among other resolutions, for Global Reparatory Justice.

It all began when I became aware of "The Black Folks Plan" as a brainchild initiated and nurtured by Chairman Hershel Daniels, Jr. The story begins with the Organization of African Unity (OAU) which was formed in 1963 as a common entity joining African countries against effects of colonialism. The OAU was re-named the African Union in 2002. At that time, the African Union opened membership opportunities to populations in the African Diaspora. By November 17, 2011, Chairman Daniels and other associates organized Friends of the African Union (FAU), representing the African (Kemetic) American diaspora, to join the African Union.

The #Black Folks Plan: How did we get here? Author, Hershel Daniels, Jr. - Amazon: Print or digital

The Friends of the African Union is an "economic, social, humanitarian, charitable, educational and new media civil society ruling body founded to work for the benefit of the people of the African Union and the African Diaspora in their host countries."

The FAU realized that the African Union was the only organization that had the structural and functional capacity to unite and service the needs and aspirations of more than 1.5 billion sons and daughters of Kemet Worldwide.

Chairman Daniels and his associates at the FAU, Brotherhood and Sisterhood International (BSI 501(c)3 1989), and Blacks and Whites Uniting Communities, formed the African Diaspora Directorate (AfDiDi) to reinforce their work in the United States. Mr. Kofi Agyapong, a Ghana national is Chairperson of AfDiDi formed as a joint venture to meet the global objectives. By 2019, the Friends of the African Union Global Operations Center and the African Diaspora Directorate announced a Global African American anti-racism stimulus program solution called the #BlackFolksPlan. Chairman Daniels prefers to describe "Black Folks" as all people of African, the Caribbean, Brazilian, the United States and global people of Kemetic descent as "Black Folk" so, I yield to this description.

The FAU and AfDiDi formed a collaborative relationship with the World Conference of Mayors, Inc., established 1987, their United Nations of Cities, and Historical Black Towns and Settlements presided by His Excellency Former Mayor Johnny Ford, Birmingham Alabama. Together, they worked their politics and were victorious in achieving the enactment of three Executive Orders signed by former President Obama, former President Trump and President Joeseph Biden. Most significant of these is:

E.O. 13985: January 20, 2022: President Joe Biden "Advancing Racial Equity and Support for Underserved Communities through the Federal Government for the pursuance of equity for all and understanding that advancing equity requires a systemic approach to embedding fairness in decision-making processes through executive departments and agencies who must recognize and work to redress inequities in their policies and programs that serve as barriers to equal opportunity."

The #Black Folks Plan p. 104

I can't pass up this opportunity for a training message. Notice how a brilliant Leader was able to galvanize – bringing together other leaders, members of organizations and individuals who came together to execute a plan. They probably did not agree on all strategies and tactics. They saw where each could collectively fit into this greater plan, combined their unique ideas and key contacts for mutual benefit. And Look What Happened? Billions with a B and Trillions with a T in a 50-year economic development plan. We cannot allow external forces of deceit and greed to invade the success of these objectives.

Guess What? Solutions Specialists!!!

First: Join for Free, the National Community Reinvestment Coalition preferably in the name of an Organization or as an Individual to access resources from the "Community Benefits Agreement." https://ncrc.org/

Second: Meet with each other and plan ahead to Save-Our-Selves. The only way to access any portion of the Billions (with a B) of dollars is to go nice and peaceful-like and in Great Mass to our Local Politicians in the name of our faith- and community-based organizations, individuals, families and neighbors and Demand that He, She, They All endorse the National Community Reinvestment Plan at the State, City, and/or County Levels. Our local Elected Representatives are able to instruct us in strategies to access statewide/local Community Benefits Agreements e.g., PNC Bank in April 2021 ($88 Billion allocated BFPlan p. 112). Ohio, Oklahoma, Georgia, Alabama, and California have already begun this process. This is also related in part, to the call for Reparations as Reparatory Justice Solutions. What are the rest of us waiting for?

The Friends of the African Union builds strategies and is structured based on the 7 Pillars of Social Justice:

1. Take care of babies, kids, and teens including when they are in school and after with an emphasis on global history, Advanced Placement (AP) Science Technology Engineering

and Math (STEAM), Fashion Arts Music Entertainment (FAME), Public Service, and, in Sports/Recreation);
2. Take care of families in distress;
3. Take care of those people involved in domestic violence;
4. Take care of those who do not have the means to feed themselves;
5. Take care of people in need of a home;
6. Take care of those people who need health care;
7. Take care of those people who need help to fulfill life as part of a new global social compact with the United States of America as expressed in the aspirations in its Declaration of Independence and evolution as a nation from March 4, 1789, the Universal Declaration of Human Rights, and as a superset of the Document of Human Fraternity for World Peace and Living together, so as to leave no one behind through the 7 Pillars of Social Justice.

The World Conference of Mayors, Inc. Committee on the Permanent Forum for People of African Descent implements the 7 T's of the World Conference of Mayors, Inc. The WCM strongly believe that leaders of local government working together can lead to a more peaceful world and facilitate economic prosperity for all.

World Conference of Mayors 7 Fundamental Goals

1. Trust
2. Trade
3. Tourism
4. Technology Transfer
5. Twin Cities (Official Collaborations for mutual Development between specific United States and African Cities.)
6. Treasury
7. Training

In response to issues of food deprivation and improved nutrition, the Black Farmers Plan Directed by Queen Mother Bernice Atchison from Chilton County, Alabama seeks to resurrect the unresolved and non-litigated "State of Black Farmers in the United States." The issues were raised during the House Agriculture Committee Hearing to Review the State of Black Farmers in the U.S. on Thursday, March 25, 2021. The Bates Justice Committee for Black Farmers, spearheaded by the World Conference of Mayors and the UN Permanent Forum of People of African Descent was formed to ensure that "E.O. 13985 and other laws are applied to the US Department of Agriculture and all of the U.S. Government to get Justice for Black American Farmers," The #Black Folks Plan p. 235

Solution Specialists worldwide, you can now formulate or bring your work into a greater reality by choosing a focus area or target population. The Black Folks Plan allows you to have a macroscopic broad view of development objectives. Cultural development allows you to view self, family, and community under a microscope. When all people everywhere apply these tools and strategies, the result will be Interdependent, Intergenerational, Intercultural Rapid Cycle Change. Take a look at the schematic diagram of the definition of culture. Locate places where you see a deficit or can apply a repair that is needed to the 7 pillars of justice or plan a project relating to the 7 Fundamental Goals.

# Culture

- The way in which man obtains

FOOD
CLOTHING
SHELTER

- The mutual relations between individuals
- The subjective behavior of man manifested in:

ART
RELIGION
ETHICS
SCIENCE

GEOGRAPHICAL ENVIRONMENT
acting through the intermediary of:

**ECONOMIC CONDITIONS** related to:

Property Concepts
Occupation
Family Organization
Religious Functions of Society
Social Functions of Society
Which Facilitate economic needs and influence economic life

Culture is unified according to definite patterns:
　　Fundamental attitudes dominate the thoughts and behavior of the society.
　　Children grow into the integrated culture largely by imitation.

Source: *The Encyclopedia of the Social Sciences, Vol. 2* (1930) from Thesis: (1985) Harris, V.L. Perceptions of the Arts Institution in the African-American Community Focus on The Muse Community Museum in Central Brooklyn: Cornell University.

## Culture Defined

Using the pretext of "international development,"- cultural development implies strategies for facilitating, training, workshops, how-to', hands-on, study, coaching, testing, improving, etc. These activities apply Globally to People of African Descent and our Allies.

In the introduction to *Resist Turbulent Times: Ways to Save-Our-Selves*, I included a description of persons and their neighbors from the "Zulu Personal Statement". I will end with a powerful quote from this profound affirmation for planning and executing projects resulting in rapid cycle change.

p. 378 *African Intellectual Heritage*, Asante & Arberry.

"I have all I need to forever be responsible.
For I am the source of all meaning, all value and all authority.
I build a Civilization in homage to the person;
The highest points reached by other civilizations are in the sky;
These zeniths are the levels from which I start building;
I entered the earth to create order out of chaos;
I recognize the person as my Light;
I pay homage to the Light;
The Light will prevail,
For I know the heights from which they made me fall;
I know the depths into which they thrust me;
I know I shall prevail,
For I am who I say I am;
He has not been born who shall say he has conquered me!"

Verda H. Olayinka
01-06-2024

# Sources

*Consciencism: Philosophy and ideology for Decolonization.*
Nkrumah, K. (1963) Monthly Review Press: New York.

*"On the theory and practice of transformational collaboration"*
Himmelman, A. T. in Huxham, C. Ed. (1996) Creating Collaborative Advantage; Sage Ch. 2

## Additional Info:

https://affinitymagazine.us/2017/03/15/the-illegal-harvesting-of-black-mens-organs-is-going-unnoticed/

https://www.ncregister.com/cna/us-house-passes-bill-to-combat-forced-organ-harvesting

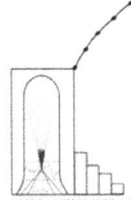

"Fear Paralyzes, Courage Mobilizes"... Wéma Ragophala

Are you ready, willing, and able to take action NOW? Assess your resources to successfully begin the process…Learn how to bring together groups…

A Society Without Ethics Cannot Grow and Evolve…It will be destined to implode upon itself!

Be a better provider… Save-Our-Selves

Let us hear from you… working the pulsating pineal pinecones… thinking, planning & doing!!!

Visit my Website!

https://www.pinealpinecones.com

https://www.SaveOurSelves.me

# ABOUT THE AUTHOR

Verda H. Olayinka has been a Lifetime Scholar in Africana Studies and a self-made student of Cultural Development. She is a former New York City Research Scientist II - Evaluator with the Department of Health and Mental Hygiene, Bureaus of HIV/AIDS and Health Care Access and Improvement.

Harris-Olayinka continued her dual career track through 2019, as Online Adjunct Professor at SUNY's Empire State College, Center for Distance Learning, as Instructor of "The United States Health Systems" and "Roots and Routes of African Diaspora Resistance."

Olayinka earned a Dual Degree in Sociology and African-American Studies from Brooklyn College in 1974. Ms. Olayinka earned a Master of Professional Studies from Cornell University in 1985 with a multidisciplinary degree in African and African American Studies and a minor concentration in Communication Arts. Her intellectual curiosity concerned the somewhat contemporary events that occurred following the mass migrations to the big cities. Communication research provided her with functional skills in Community Research and the Psychology of Behavior and Attitude Change.

This gave rise to a cumulative forty years in Human Services Management in public health, integrated health care for family and community well-being. Ms. Olayinka honed her expertise via community-based initiatives, which enhanced her understanding of the challenges of documenting effective program planning, development, and implementation.

Ms. Verda Olayinka recognizes (2022) The #Black Folks Plan, written by Chairman Hershel Daniels, Jr., to be the perfect parallel policy enactment to activate the essential keys to energize marching orders for Solutions Specialists all over the World. Friends of the African Union has been paving the way to activate and empower this new strategy for Sons and Daughters of Kemet (Africa) to "Save-Our-Selves, One-By-One and All-Together."

www.ingramcontent.com/pod-product-compliance
Lightning Source LLC
Chambersburg PA
CBHW042114100526
44587CB00025B/4053